EMPERICISM
CLASSICAL AND CONTEMPORARY

Supriya Saha

RAJAT PUBLICATIONS
New Delhi

Empericism: Classical and Contemporary
by *Supriya Saha*

This edition is published by Rajat Publications
4740/23, Ansari Road Daryaganj,
New Delhi - 110002

ISBN: 978-81-7880-251-0

Edition 2025

Rs. 1395/-

Printed and bound in India

RAJAT
PUBLICATIONS

4740/23, Ansari Road, Daryaganj,
New Delhi- 110002 (India)
Mob:- +91-9811484973, +91-9811105389
E-mail: rajat_publication@yahoo.com

Dedicated
To My Beloved Parents
Dr. P.G. Pal & Smt. Deepti K. Pal

PREFACE

The present work offers a comparative study of the epistemological and ontological doctrines of David Hume (1711-76) and A.J. Ayer (1910-1989). Both, Hume and Ayer are the most outstanding representatives of classical and contemporary linguistic empiricism respectively. Whereas Hume brings to a logical culmination the empiricism of Locke and Berkeley, Ayer in his logical positivism, revives Hume's epistemological and ontological premises by using what he calls a "developed and sophisticated logical technique". The "logical technique" of Ayer consists in his use of a formal mode of speech through which he verbally manoeuvres the central philosophical doctrines of Humc's empiricism. Hume's empiricism, practised for over a century, thus seems to have a remarkable influence on the philosophical thinking of Ayer. It is for this reason, that I have selected the philosophies of David Hume and A.J. Ayer, for a comparative study.

There are two alternative ways of analysing these philosophers. One way is to analyse and examine their philosophies within the framework of empiricistic or linguistic philosophy respectively. The other alternative consists of stepping out of the empiricistic and linguistic framework and then analyse their philosophical viewpoints.

I have tried to examine the philosophies of Hume

and Ayer from both the above mentioned perspectives.

My aim in this study does not consist simply in cataloguing the resemblances and differences between Hume and Ayer. The present study lies in mutual supplementation of arguments and consequent clarification of issues, thereby helping the growth of philosophical heritage.

Hume claims that our knowledge deals only with the "facts" which can be known through "impressions and ideas" alone. This implies that for him, no propositions can be considered as true, unless it is given in sense experience, in the form of impressions and ideas. So, for Hume sense-experience, is a 'criterion of knowledge'. Ayer, on the other hand claims that no sentence is even "meaningful", unless something corresponding to it is observable-directly or indirectly. So, we find that Ayer converts, Hume's `criterion of truth' into a "criterion of meanining". Thus, whereas Hume emphasises on the knowledge of "facts", through sense-experience, Ayer claims to give importance to the "meaning" of a proposition on the basis of sense-experience. This implies that Hume advocates a specific epistemology and ontology in his philosophy, whereas Ayer claims to confine himself only to logic and semantics.

However, in spite of their apparently different professed objectives, it seems that the arguments that are used by Hume in order to defend his position are also adapted by Ayer, in a logico-linguistic framework to suit his empiricistic requirements. I have attempted to analyse and interpret their philosophies by following a historico-analytic methodology.

Following the above mentioned methodology I, in this study, have tried to trace Hume and Ayer historically and have highlighted the fact that their philosophies can be said to be a continuation of the mental side of the Cartesian dualism, through the empiricism of Berkeley. I have also tried to show that by denying the material substance and consequently the 'objective material reality', both Hume and Ayer reject the arguments, which are respectively used by Descartes (rationalist) and Locke, in attempting to assert the existence of the external material reality. This work, thus introduces the readers to the basic tenets of Descartes, Locke, Berkeley and Hume. It is analytic because it helps to make certain clarifications regarding both these philosophers. For instance our analysis reveal, in the context of Hume, that although he claims to deal with "facts", (impressions) which, according to him, exist independently of a mental and material substance, he actually deals with `sensations'. And since, sensations cannot be separated from the individuals who receive them we find that Hume's position can be interpreted to be close to that of Berkeley's. As a result, although most of his exponents regard him to be a realist, I have made an attempt to show that Hume can also be interpreted as a subjective-idealist philosopher.

The above interpretation also holds valid, in the context of Ayer. Ayer claims that only "neutral" "sense-data" or "sense-contents" are verifiable. He reduces the meaning of propositions to a testification by the occurrence of these "sense-data" or "sense-contents" in one's sense-experience. It appears to me that these "sense-data" are nothing but one's own `sensations'. So, what Ayer calls "neutral sense-contents", seems to have the same mental status as that of Hume's "impressions"

As a result, although Ayer is regarded as a linguistic analyst, by most philosophers, we find that, on the basis of the status of his "sense-data" or "sense-contents", his position comes close to Berkeley's subjective-idealist position.

Since Hume's "impressions" and Ayer's "sense-data" are nothing but 'objects of sensations', in their philosophy, there seems to be an absolutisation of only one aspect of the concrete totality, namely the 'sensations' (in the form of "impressions" in Hume and "sense-contents" in Ayer). These impressions and sense-data are mere 'appearances'. As a result, we find that there can be no internal relations among the particular appearances, in the ontology of Hume and Ayer. Hence we find a subsequent denial of the category of the necessary causal connections in both these philosophers. In a nutshell, I would like to point out, that both Hume and Ayer deny the categories of scientific investigation. In the pretext of eliminating metaphysics, they can thus be regarded as advocating a metaphysical approach in their epistemology and ontology. (Here "Metaphysics" implies taking in isolation one aspect of reality and absolutising it).

It is further observed that by accepting only the "impressions" and "sense-data", these philosophers while denying the `objective reality' logically deny the existence of independent objective value-structure. This is because, Hume says that only those statements are knowable and hence meaningful, which are either statements of "relations of ideas" or that of "matters of fact". So, for him not only the metaphysical statements but also value statements (which include both the aesthetic and moral values), become meaningless.

Similarly, according to Ayer, only "analytic" and "synthetic" propositions are meaningful. Analytic propositions are meaningful because they are "tautologies" and synthetic propositions are meaningful because they are "verifiable". Therefore, even for Ayer, metaphysical statements as well as value-statements are not meaningful.

It seems to us that the denial of objective moral value structure is a logical corollary to the proposition that there is no objective reality, which is apparent from the philosophies of Hume and Ayer. All values for them are 'subjective' values. Therefore, moral values for Hume, are a question of instinct or passions and Ayer asserts that moral statements only evinces our emotions. (This is evident from his "emotive theory" of meaning.)

I feel that a practical consequence of the denial of reality is that if there is no objective material reality, then logically, there is no possibility of transforming the objective reality. This is because, in the absence of an objective reality man is incapable of acquiring knowledge through theory and practice. He is also unable to concretise his ideas, plan his future, and generally aspire in real life situtions.

While attempting to execute the scientific methodology, in order to trace the ontological and epistemological foundations of David Hume and A.J. Ayer, the entire book has been divided into five main chapters which takes off from the second chapter after following an introduction in the first chapter.

The second chapter entitled "Development of classical Empiricism from Descartes' Dualism" gives an introductory background to the philosophies of Hume and Ayer. In this chapter, I have dealt with the central themes of the philosophical systems of Descartes, Locke, and Berkeley. I have tried to show that the roots of modern classical and contemporary linguistic-empiricism lies in the mental side of the Cartesian dualism.

The third chapter of the thesis gives an Exposition of the Epistemology and Ontology of David Hume. Here, by using the historico-analytic approach, I have traced the roots of Hume's empiricisim from the empiricistic premises of Locke and Berkeley. We have also shown that Hume can be interpreted as a subjective-idealist, by stating forward the realist-idealist polemic.

In the fourth chapter of the book, I have discussed the epistemology and ontology of A.J. Ayer, within his semantic framework. And, irrespective of his professed objectives, I have tried to trace the foundations of his philosophy, from the world-view as propounded by Hume.

The fifth chapter of the work, discusses Hume's and Ayer's Concept of Causation. I have tried to show that their denial of necessary causal connections is dialectically linked with their pluralist, subjective-idealist empiricist ontology. And, precisely for this reason, knowledge for them, is only "probable" and not certain.

Finally, in the concluding chapter of the book, I have compared Hume and Ayer. We have tried to bring into light the fact that how the results obtained by using a false methodology, as has been done by both of them stand in glaring contradiction, with actual scientific proof.

I am geatly indebted to my honourable supervisor

Professor Suman Gupta of Jawaharlal Nehru University, New Delhi whose constant encouragement, stimulating ideas, criticisms and expostulation provided an impetus for attempting to accomplish the present work.

Also my deep debt of gratitude goes to Dr. Raghavendra Pratap Singh of Jawaharlal Nehru University, New Delhi for his invaluable advocacy.

My most heart felt appreciation goes to my parents, whose love and self-sacrifice will always be an inspiration to me. At the same time, I also extend my utmost respect to my mother-in-law and to my other family members for their unflinching assistance and cooperation in all aspects. I will always remember the tangible help provided by my sister and brother.

Last but not the least I should also thank my husband, Mr. Debabrata Saha and my daughter Miss Aarushi Saha who supported me in all possible manner to complete the present work.

—Supriya Saha

CONTENTS

1

INTRODUCTION

History of philosophy has largely evolved and developed around the problem of appearance and reality. This is a crucial issue in philosophy because an understanding of the 'apparent' and the 'real' is significant in determining the epistemological and ontological positions of a philosopher. Moreover, it also has relevance in our day to day life and experiences.

Our reflection on certain instances of daily life reveal that things are not always what they seem to be. To take a simple but reccuring example, a stick which appears straight looks bent when immersed in water. Such an instance points to the distinction between the apparent and the real. Everything in this world is therefore said to have two aspects i.e. an external aspect which is always changing and an internal aspect, unseen from outside, which remains unchanged amidst changes in the external forms. This unchangeable aspect of a thing therefore needs to be explained and the problem of appearance and reality is not to be dismissed as an abstract issue.

Philosophers since ancient times till the present day are unanimous in naming this unchangeable aspect as the "substance". However at the same time, they are varied in their opinions regarding the status of "substance" i.e. to say whether "substance" is given in the phenomenal world, or it belongs to the transcendental world.

Some of the philosophers, particularly those having a metaphysical approach (e.g. ancient Greek philosophers and medieval philosophers) maintain that "substance" is transcendental in nature. Infact reality itself is transcendental for these philosophers. As for example, we find in Plato's philosophical system that he gives importance to the "world of forms" rather than the phenomenal world and thus tries to divert the attention of the people from the actual reality to the other world which is beyond human understanding. Similarly, thinkers of the medieval period, namely St. Thomas Aquinas, St. Augustine etc, consider God as the only substance, only reality and explain everything with the help of God.

In fact it is observed that to some extent partly the Greek philosophers and partly the medieval philosophers were responsible to convey to the common man that philosophy deals with nothing but absractions, god, theology and so on. Nevertheless the contribution of these philosophers to the history of ideas is not to be underestimated. Today, there is a remarkable progress in the development of philosophy and this has been achieved largely by way of interpretaion and analysis of old ideas, concepts and theories.

Generations after generations, philosophers have busied themselves in attempting to overcome the shortcomings which have figured in their preeceeding philosophical systems, in the light of their prevailing social conditions.

This has led to reconstruction of old theories into new ones and consequent formation of new concepts in philosophy. I have tried to highlight this aspect of philosophical development in this book. In the process I have tried to show how classical empiricism grew and developed out of rationalism (Decartes dualism) and how contemporary empiricism (Logical positivism of Ayer) emerged out of Hume's empiricism. This is precisely how the scope and aim of philosophy has changed over the years thus showing progress in the sphere of human thinking.

Today attempts are being made to make philosophy even more rigorous and scientific by denying certain branches of speculation (e.g. metaphysics) in philosophy. The philosophical systems of Hume and Ayer are pointers towards this direction. However it remains to be seen how far these philosophers have succeeded in making philosophy scientific by propagating an anti meta-physical approach.

The anti-metaphysical attitude is evident in Hume when he asserts that there are only two kinds of meaningul propositions namely "Relations of ideas" and "matters of fact". This is reflected in his following quoted line. "If we take in our hand any volume, of divinity or school meta-physics, for instance; let us ask, does it contain any abstract reasoning concerning quantity or number? No. Does it contain any experimental reasoning concerning matter of fact and existence? No. Commit it then to the flames, for it can contain nothing but sophistry and illusion."

The above mentioned attitude of Hume is further carried on in contemporary thinking by Ayer, when the latter holds that all literally meaningful propositions exhaust themselves between "analytic" and "synthetic" propositions.

Here it needs to be mentioned that both these philosophers had different reasons for their respective anti-speculative attitudes. In case of Hume it is attributed to his attempt to bring classical empiricism of Locke and Berkeley to its logical culmination. On the other hand where Ayer is concerned the anti-meta-physical tendency is due to the excessive preoccupation of the contemporary philosophers with linguistic analysis which also includes lot of logico-mathematical elements in it. So the philosophical pre-occupations of Hume and Ayer seem to be different, yet it is remarkable how Ayer in his logical positivism adopts the basic tenets of Hume, which were practised by him in the eighteenth century.

Being essentially empricists both these philosophers in contrast to Greek and medieval philosophers attempt to explain "substance" empirically and conclude that substance-material or spiritual is not a reality. According to them "substance" is only a fiction of the mind and all that exist are the qualities in the form of sense-impressions (in case of Hume) and sense data (in case of Ayer). Reality for these philosophers is therefore sensations (constituted of sense-impressions and sense-data) each of which is separate and discreet entity.

Consequently, Hume expresses that any knowledge in order to be real must have elements corresponding to some impressions. So he argues that the knowledge of substance must also be traced from some sense-impressions-either sensations or reflections. But he fails to do so. Therefore he interprets the idea of a substance to be a collection of simple ideas, united by imagination, which have a common name assigned to it. He further extends this argument in order to reduce the spiritual substance or the "self" to a "bundle of perceptions".

Following Hume Ayer also explains that both the material and the mental substances can be defined only in terms of sense-contents, because it is only by the occurrence of certain sense contents that their existence can be verified at the least degree. So we observe that both Hume and Ayer reduce "substance" to a mere assemblage of sense-impressions and sense-contents respectively. In other words "substance" is reduced to a collection of sensations in the philosophies of Hume and Ayer and in the process the distinction between appearance and reality is abolished by these philosophers.

Irrespective of their claims, we know that even though "substance" is not given directly to our sense-experience its existence needs to be admitted. This is because "substance" forms the substratum of the qualities and properties which we observe in the objects around us. Besides "substance" also constitutes an important and indespesable category of knowledge. Other categories of knowledge for e.g. causality, necessity and so on are dependent on the category of substance. Finally it is observed that in the history of philosophy those philosophers who have supported the existence of "substance" have also asserted necessary causal connections among the various aspects of reality and consequently stressed on the fact that knowledge is certain (for e.g. Descartes). On the other hand philosophers who have advanced a reductive analysis of the category of "substance" (like Hume and Ayer) have failed to explain necessary causal connections and consequently expressed that knowledge is only probable. Thus "substance" constitute an instrumental category in determining the ontological postion of a philosopher (Dualism is case of Descartes and pluralism in case of Hume and Ayer).

As far as the anti meta-physical attitude in Hume and Ayer is concerned an important question arises namely that is having an anti-metaphysical approach analogous to having a scientific approach. I want to mention here that the term "metaphysics" should not be taken to convey just one connotation i.e., dealing with supersensible reality. There are several sensesof this term which I have mentioned in this book. One such sense of the term "metaphysics" is to take one aspect of reality from its totality and to absolutize it and in this respect both Hume and Ayer can be said to harbouring metaphysical interests since they have only tried to absolutize the "sensations".

Knowledge on the other hand is social in nature. Its growth and progress is ensured not only by mere sensations but also by reason as is expressed by Kant. In fact knowledge is a joint venture of several aspects of reality like the objective and the subjective, the apparent and the real, theory and practice, abstract and concrete, form and content and so on and it is only in a correct methodology that we find an inter connection between all these aspects of reality. This is what constitutes the scientific methedology.

Viewed from this perspective it is observed that the one sided approach of Hume and Ayer not only make them mataphysicians but the results achieved through such an approach are contrary to results achieved through a scientific approach.

2

DEVELOPMENT OF CLASSICAL EMPIRICISM FROM DESCARTES' DUALISM

In this chapter, we have discussed the development of classical empiricism and the studies are based on the following methodological assumptions:

(1) "...a distinction between what a philosopher claims to be doing and what he is actually doing.

(2) ...that every philosophical position presupposes a world-view, i.e., a specific ontology and epistemology.

(3) ...that in a consistent philosophical system ontology and epistemology are logically interdependent."[1]

Following the above mentioned methodological assumptions, We in this chapter, have mainly dealt with the epistemology and ontology of Rene Descartes', John Locke and Bishop Berkeley. This shall serve as an introductory background to the philosophies of David Hume and A.J. Ayer who are being considered in the following chapters of this book and in analysing Hume and Ayer we have executed the same methodology.

In order to understand the epistemological and ontological implications of the philosophers concerned in this chapter as well as later in the book, we have firstly analysed their views on knowledge from the point of view of the three components of knowledge namely, the subject, the object and the source, as they conceive it. An examination of the various components of knowledge contributes to a better understanding of a particular philosophical system. Once the subject, the object and the source of knowledge are isolated from one another, it is easier to see, how various philosophers conceive their nature so that if needed one can reformulate them within the framework of the specific philosophical system which one wants to analyse.

Secondly, we have adopted the historical approach. The significance of historical approach lies in unravelling the "unstated assumptions" which a philosopher takes into consideration while constructing his own systems of thought. This is explained by Suman Gupta in this manner.... "*To capture correctly the nature of the subject and the object of knowledge as conceived by a specific philosopher it is essential to take into account both the stated as well as the unstated assumptions into consideration and to dig out the underlying unstated assumptions it is furthermore essential to adopt the historical approach. The adoption of historical approach is essential because most of the philosophers while developing their own philosophical system take for granted some of the basic assumptions of their predecessors.*"[2]

By executing the aforementioned methodological

assumptions, and the historical approach we have attempted to fathom the assumptions of Hume and Ayer, which have been traced from Descartes', Locke and Berkeley, And in doing so we have tried to show through relevant arguements, how not only classical empiricism but also contemporary empiricism (of Ayer in this book), in spite of their respective claims, take for granted the mental side of cartesian dualism. Hence let us begin the discussion by explaining Cartesian Dualism.

CARTESIAN DUALISM

Dualism, in common parlance asserts that there are two fundamental realities, namely, mind and matter, which exist separately and, that neither of these realities can be reduced to the other.

In modern philosophy, dualism, as stated by Descartes (1596-1650) is known as the "Cartesian dualism". Descartes also maintains that mind and matter are two independent realities. But, being a rationalist, he claims that it is easier to know the mind than the body or matter. He writes, "*...the mind, by which I am what I am, is entirely distinct from the body, and even that it is easier to know than the body, and moreover, that even if the body were not, it would not cease to be all that it is.*"[3] Thus Descartes gives primacy to mind over body or matter. Although he claims "dualism" to be the last step of his "methodic doubt", it appears that dualism constitutes the first step of his philosophy. In other words, we have tried to argue that he already assumes dualism and therefore it is mandatory to examine Descartes' original claims, which are stated by him in his methodic doubt.

METHODIC DOUBT

Descartes begins his methodic doubt with the assumption that there is some certain knowledge about the world which must be self-evident. He makes his position clear when he writes, "I had long ago noticed that in matters relating to conduct, one needs sometimes to follow, just as if they were indubitable, opinions one knows to be very unsure; ".... *but as I wanted to concentrate solely on the search for truth, I thought I ought to do just the opposite, and reject as being absolutely false anything in which I could suppose the slightest reason for doubt, in order to see if there did not remain after that anything in my belief which was entirely indubitable.*"[4]

It follows, according to Descartes that one can systematically arrive at a single, certain truth, only through deliberate doubt. He disclaims the source of sense-testimony in his search for truth, because according to him, our senses deceive us at times as in the case of illusions, hallucinations etc. "*But I have sometimes found that these senses played me false, and it is prudent never to trust entirely those who have once deceived us.*"[5] He further writes in the *Discourse*, ".... *and because there are men who make mistakes in reasoning, even with the simplest geometrical matters, I rejected as being false all the reasoning I had hitherto accepted as proofs.*"[6] *Thus Descartes seems to refuse all sorts of mathematical or geometrical reasoning in his search for certainty. On the other hand, he proposes that when doubt is pushed to its farthest limit, it reveals something which is not only indubitable, but is also clearly perceived; and that is the doubter who doubts and thus thinks.* *He thereby writes,* ".... *I resolved to pretend that nothing which had entered my mind was any more true than the illusions of my dreams. But immediately afterwards I become aware that, while I decided thus to think that everything was false, it followed necessarily, that I who thought thus must be something; and observing that this truth: I think, therefore I am, was so certain and so evident that all the most extravagant suppositions of the sceptics were not capable of shaking it, I judged that I could accept it without scruple as the first principle of the philosophy I was seeking.*"[7]

In this way, through methodic doubt, Descartes lays claim to the attainment of the first final certainty in his system. I think, therefore I am or to use his own language, *Cogito ergo sum* thus constitutes the first principle - the first necessarily true proposition of his philosophy. He writes in the *Second Meditation*, "*.... after having thought carefully about it, and having scrupulously examined everything, one must then, in conclusion, take as assured that the proposition. I am, I exist, is necessarily true, every time I express it or conceive of it in my mind.* "[8]

'Cogito' thus implies the attribute of thinking or consciousness in his philosophy. In other words, he seems to derive his existence from his thinking. "*I am, I exist: this is certain, but for how long? For as long as I think, for it might perhaps happen, if I ceased to think, that I would at the same time cease to be or to exist.*"[9] So, it ensues that for Descartes there is no other function apart from the conscious function which can guarantee the existence of the self. This is evident when he says that it would not be correct to say "I walk therefore I am", because walking without being conscious cannot imply self-existence.

Consequently he arrives at the indubitable truth of the inseparability of thought and thing. *"I am, however, a real thing, and really existing: but what thing? ....A thing which thinks."*[10]

This 'thinking thing', constitutes the mental substance in Descartes philosophy. It is thus apparent that he already assumes the existence of the mental substance. *"I thereby concluded that I was a substance, of which the whole essence or nature consists in thinking."*[11]

The mental substance or the thinking thing or the self is one which, according to him, thinks, doubts, imagines, senses, desires etc. *"What is a thing that thinks? That is to say, a thing that doubts, perceives, affirms, denies, wills, does not will, that imagines also, and which feels."*[12] Beyond these activities he maintains, *"I am not this assemblage of limbs called the human body."*[13] We thus find that Descartes tends to isolate all the activities, which also constitute ones consciousness from their very physical and biological base. Therefore he is interpreted to be different from other philosophers. In his system "Cogito" thus expresses nothing but pure consciousness.

But our day to day observations show that there is nothing as 'pure consciousness'. This is because, the various activities of consciousness like thinking, willing etc. cannot take place apart from a corresponding biological organ which is nothing but part of a body. Hence it appears that Descartes assumes the material substance. Therefore, it has been observed by some philosophers that dualism is his first step although he claims it to be the last step of his methodic doubt.

Coming back to the 'Cogito', since this constitutes a self-evident proposition, he expresses that it is also clear and distinct and therefore true. As a result, he makes a general rule that all things which are clearly and distinctly perceived are true. *"And having noticed that there is nothing at all in this, I think, therefore I am, which assures me that I am speaking the truth, except that I see very clearly that in order to think one must exist, I judged that I could take it to be a general rule that the things we conceive very clearly and very distinctly are all true."*[14] So Descartes derives the criterion of truth from the certainty of 'cogito ergo sum'. On the basis of the truth of the 'cogito', he further makes an attempt to examine all such ideas which can be proved to be true. But at the same time he explains that no idea can be certain as long as we are confronted with the notion of a deceiving God. Therefore, he classifies all ideas into three categories:

(a) those which are innate.

(b) those derived from outside and

(c) those which are our own inventions.

Of these ideas, he holds that there is only one such innate idea of God which is eternal, infinite and perfect. But then there must be some cause of this idea of God. According to him this cause cannot be the individual consciousness because it is finite and not completely perfect. In this context he writes, *"I could not make... judgement concerning the idea of a being more perfect than myself... because it is no less contradictory that the more perfect should proceed from and depend on the less perfect, than it is that something should emerge out of nothing, I could not hold it from myself.*"[15] As a result, he deduces the consciousness of God from the conception of an absolutely perfect being. *"...it must have been put into me by a being whose nature was truly more perfect than mine and which even had in itself all the perfection of which I could not have any idea, that is to say, in a single word, which was God ... there must of necessity be another more perfect, upon whom I depended, and from whom I had acquired all I had.*"[16] In this way Descartes asserts that the idea of Infinite perfect Being is clear and distinct, because it is only in comparison with the fullness of the Perfect Being that we realise our finitude. The idea of God is therefore, a clear and distinct idea in his ontology. It is once again observed that by asserting the existence of God, he emphasizes on 'pure consciousness'.

Apart from the idea of God, he explains, at the same time, that we also experience ideas such as of colour, taste, smell as well as the feelings of pleasure, pain, etc. He says that we imagine that these must be caused by bodies outside of us, but we cannot rely on their existence through our senses as our senses deceive us. Neither, does he hold that we can, ourselves produce these ideas. So, he concludes that they must be produced either by God or by the things outside. But if these ideas are produced by God, then God must be a deceiver, for we are not aware that he is their cause. But he says that God is not a deceiver. Hence he opines that these ideas must be caused by real bodies and corresponding to this clear and distinct perception, he settles that there must be an external world of bodies. *"....for perception by the senses is very obscured and confused in many ways; but at least I must admit that all that I conceive clearly and distinctly... all that is comprised in the object of speculative geometry, is truly to be found in corporeal things.... I may conclude with assurance that I have within me the means of knowing these things with certainty."*[17] Thus the existence of the corporeal things or the material substance as a clear and distinct idea is established in his philosophy. As stated by him, the essential attribute of a corporeal substance consists in its being extended, which is perceived clearly and distinctly. *"I recognize .... in myself certain other faculties, such as changing place, of adopting various postures.... But it is very evident that these faculties if it be true that they exist, must be attached to some corporeal or extended substance, and not to an intelligent substance, since in their clear and distinct concept there is indeed contained some sort of extension, but no intellection at all."*[18]

It is thus derived that the way "consciousness" forms an essential attribute of mind, "extension" constitutes the essential attribute of matter, in Descartes ontology. But where material objects are concerned, we also perceive certain qualities in them such as colour, taste, etc. Hence a question arises, how does he explain these qualities?

In his attempt to accommodate the above mentioned qualities Descartes classifies all of them into primary and secondary types. According to him, primary qualities are the attributes of the body as we "perceive them clearly and distinctly". These include extension, figure, motion, number, rest and duration. Of these, he holds that only extension constitutes the main attribute of the body because it can exist on its own whereas figure, motion etc. are all modes of extension, as they are dependent on it.

The secondary qualities on the other hand, according to him, are the confused ideas present in the perceiver's mind. He says we "do not perceive them clearly and distinctly". Consequently, they do not form the attributes of the body. According to him, the qualities of colour, taste etc. belongs to this category. He maintains that these confused ideas, give rise to "error" when we give our assent or dissent to them, whereas there is no room for error in case of clear ideas.

The aforementioned distinction between the primary and secondary qualities is accepted in toto by Locke, and this has been shown in the next sections.

Coming back to Descartes', It follows, from the above discussion that one can have clear and distinct ideas of both the mental as well as material substance in his ontology. Mind and Matter are two relative substances for him, which though independent of one another depend for their existence on God. So, God constitutes the absolute substance for Descartes.

It may be mentioned here that the category of substance has important philosophical implications in determining the epistemology of a philosopher.

In the history of philosophy we find that those philosophers who assert this category regard knowledge to be certain, universal and necessary, and those who deny it, subsequently deny certain knowledge. As we have stated Descartes assumes certain knowledge, therefore he accepts the category of substance in his ontology. Similarly, we have attempted to bring out in the context of Locke, that he too aims at certain knowledge and therefore accepts

Descartes' dualism in order to account for the category of material substance; This of course has given rise to inconsistencies in his philosophy which we have dealt with later. On the other hand, we have tried to show that Hume and Ayer both deny the category of substance. Hence, knowledge for them is only "probable" and not certain.

Regarding the mental and material substance of Descarte's, he on the basis of their essential attributes, namely, "consciousness" and "extension" respectively, propounds that mind and body are diametrically opposed to each other. Thus he writes, "*.... on the one hand, I have a clear and distinct idea of myself in so far as I am only a thinking and unextended thing, and, ...on the other hand I have a distinct idea of the body in so far as it is only an extended thing but which does not think, it is certain that I, that is to say my mind, ...entirely and truly distinct from any body and may exist without it.*"[19] This comprises the "mind-body" dualism in Descartè's system which he professes to be the last step of his methodic doubt.

From Descartes dualism, with the further assumption that mind is prior to body it logically follows that his ontological and epistemological position is an idealistic one. But since he accepts body or matter to be an independent reality, it is also conveyed that he advocates materialism. In this connection Suman Gupta writes, "*In the history of modern western philosophy Descartes was the first philosopher who while accepting the existence of both consciousness (mind) and matter (body) completely divorced one from the other. And Descartes' dualism gave birth to two diametrically opposed metaphysical systems, namely, (1) subjective idealism, (2) mechanical materialism. Each of them accept in the absolute metaphysical sense only one side of Cartesian dualism, i.e., the subjective idealist accept only consciousness and mechanical materialists accept only matter. When logically analysed, we find the three basic assumptions of Cartesian dualism constitutes the ontological foundations of subjective idealist epistemology.*"[20]

Following Descartes dualism, whereas Locke accepted both the sides of Cartesian dualism, Berkeley, accepts only the 'subjective idealist' aspect of it and Hume and Ayer reject both the sides of cartesian dualism and are therefore broadly regarded as realist philosophers..

To summarise the three epistemological components in Descartes' philosophy namely, subject, object and source, we perceive that for him the subject of knowledge is the "Cogito or pure consciousness, the objects of knowledge are the true ideas representing the `objective material reality', and the source is the rational understanding of the clearness and distinctness of ideas. His position thus appears to be a "metaphysical" one because he takes the subject of knowledge in isolation from its concrete social reality and also isolates the rational aspect of knowledge from its empirical aspect and by taking rest or motion as qualities of matter, he separates matter from motion.

Let us now discuss the epistemology and ontology of John Locke.

JOHN LOCKE (1632-1704)

Locke is the first empiricist in the modern times, who advocates empiricism in the form of dualism. Even though he is an empiricist he accepts some of the assumptions of Cartesian dualism. But by accepting the assumptions of Cartesian dualism and at the same time advocating empiricism he lands himself in a number of contradictions. In order to see his influence on Hume and Ayer, we shall now give an account of his epistemology and ontology.

LOCKE'S EPISTEMOLOGY AND ONTOLOGY

In his epistemology, Locke advocates empiricism as opposed to the rationalism of Descartes'. In support of empiricism he asserts that the mind in the beginning is an "empty slate" or "tabula rasa" which he claims, can be furnished only through sense-experience. "*...How comes it to be furnished?... Whence has it all the materials of reason and knowledge? To this I answer in one word, from experience: in that all our knowledge is founded and from that it ultimately derives itself.*"[21] Thus experience accounts for the source of knowledge in Locke's philosophy. But now the question arises - what do we know from experience - do we know the ideas or the material objects?

Following descartes' dualism, he takes for granted that mind can know only its ideas, and holds that through sense experience we can directly know only our own ideas. These ideas, according to him represent the qualities and since the qualities, for their existence, require a support or substratum, Locke assumes the existence of material substance in his ontology. In fact he claims that material substance is the cause of these ideas and thus, he advances the causal theory of perception in his philosophy. But when it is asked what is the nature of the material substance he maintains that it is "unknown and unknowable".

For Locke there are two sources of knowledge i.e.,

(two kinds of experiences) namely, sensations and reflections. Through sensations, he holds that the mind gets the ideas of sensible qualities, *"First, our senses, conversant about particular sensible objects, do convey into the mind several distinct perceptions of things.... And thus we come by those ideas we have of yellow, white, heat, cold... and all those which we call sensible qualities.... This great source of most of our ideas we have, depending wholly upon our senses, and derived by them to the understanding, I call sensation."*[22] On the other hand, reflections, according to him convey to the mind, ideas of its own operations such as perception, thinking, believing etc. *"By 'REFLECTION' then... I would be understood to mean that notice which the mind takes of its own operations"*[23] He further maintains that sensations and reflections together produce the simple ideas in the mind. *"These simple ideas the materials of all our knowledge, are suggested and furnished to mind only by those two ways... viz., sensation and reflection."*[24]

It follows that in Locke's system it is the simple ideas which constitute the raw materials for our knowledge. Consequently, he defines knowledge as the "perception" of these ideas. *"Since the mind in all its thought and reasoning hath no other immediate object but its own ideas, which it alone can contemplate, it is evident that our knowledge is only conversant about them.... Knowledge then seems to me to be nothing but the perception of the connection and agreement or disagreement or repugnancy of any of our ideas. In this alone it consists."*[25]

Out of these simple ideas, Locke holds that the mind, through its various operations produce the complex ideas. *"When the understanding is once stored with these simple ideas, it has the power to repeat, compare and unite them, and so make new complex ideas.*"[26] Thus, we observe that although the simple ideas constitute the materials of knowledge for Locke, both the simple and the complex ideas form the contents of mind in his philosophy.

He further explains that through the simple ideas we apprehend qualities, thus making a distinction between ideas on the one hand and qualities on the other. "*Whatsoever the mind perceives in itself, or is the immediate object of perception thought or understanding, that I call idea; and the power to produce any idea in our mind I call quality of the subject wherein that power is.*"[27] These qualities according to him are of two kinds, namely, primary qualities and secondary qualities.

Of these qualities, the primary qualities are those which are utterly inseparable from their bodies. According to him, these are qualities which produce the simple ideas in us, "*Qualities thus considered in bodies are... utterly inseparable from the body.... These I call original or primary qualities of body, which I think we may observe to produce simple ideas in us i.e., solidity, extension, figure, motion, rest and number.*"[28] On the other hand, he expresses that the secondary qualities are nothing in the objects themselves, but powers to produce various sensations in us by their primary qualities such as colours, sounds, tastes etc. "*...such qualities which in truth are nothing in the objects themselves but powers to produce various sensations in us by their primary qualities i.e., by the bulk, figure... as colours, sound, tastes. These I call secondary qualities.*"[29]

The above statement of Locke implies that primary

qualities are resemblances of bodies whereas the secondary qualities are not so. "*that the ideas of primary qualities of bodies are resemblances of them and their patterns do really exist in the bodies themselves; but the ideas produced in us by these secondary qualities have no resemblance of them at all there is nothing like our ideas existing in the bodies themselves.*"[30]

Thus Locke makes a distinction between the primary and the secondary qualities and since the primary qualities are inseparable from the bodies he holds that they are the real qualities. "*The particular bulk, number, figure and motion of the part of fire or snow are really in them, whether any one's senses perceive them or not; and therefore they may be called real qualities because they really exist in those bodies. But light, heat, whiteness, coldness, are no more really in them than sickness or pain is in manna. Take away the sensation of them; let not the eyes see light or colours, nor the ears hear sounds; ...and all colours...sounds, as they are such particular ideas, vanish and cease, and are reduced to their causes i.e., bulk, figure, motion of parts.*"[31]

It appears from the above statement that Locke gives objective existence to the primary qualities and the bodies they inhere in. On the other hand he maintains that secondary qualities are subjective and relative. In this context he argues that the secondary qualities cannot exist in the bodies themselves because this will lead to contradiction. He explains his position in the following manner, through the example of fire. He writes, "*...it would by most men be judged very extravagant if one should say otherwise. And yet he that will consider that the same fire that at one* *distance produces in us the far distant sensation of pain, ought to bethink himself what reason he has to say that his idea of warmth, which was produced in him by the fire, is actually in the fire, and his idea of pain, which the same fire produced in him the same way, is not in the fire. Why are whiteness and coldness in snow, and pain not, when it produces the one and the other idea in us; and can neither but by the bulk, figure... of its solid parts?*"[32]

Thus Locke expresses that we cannot have both the qualities of warmth and pain in the fire itself. He assumes that material substances having primary qualities are the causes of our ideas. But as stated earlier he insists that we cannot know the material substance. This is so, because, according to him, all that we can be directly aware of, are the simple ideas. The idea of substance for him is a complex idea. It is only a 'supposition' of an unknown substratum of the simple ideas or the simple qualities which are represented by these simple ideas. "*...if anyone will examine himself concerning his notion of pure substance in general, he will find he has no other idea of it at all, but only a supposition of he knows not what support of such qualities which are capable of producing simple ideas in us....*"[33] According to him the idea of substance is a complex idea and "powers" in the form of qualities "make a great part of.... complex ideas of substance" although he describes the material substance as supposed I-know-not-what. There is thus a separation between knowledge of material substance and its existence in Locke's ontology.

This position of Locke gives rise to inconsistencies and contradictions within his own epistemological and ontological position. It is said that if we know only the simple ideas then how can we go beyond the simple ideas and draw a distinction between the ideas of the primary and secondary qualities. Secondly, it is said that if only simple ideas are given then how can material objects with primary qualities be their causes.

Locke has been criticised on this point, by many philosophers. We may mention here about Maurice Cornforth, who while criticising Locke writes, *"On the one hand, he could be criticised in that, having said that knowledge was limited to the world of our own ideas, he nevertheless allowed ideas to be represented as the product of...external objects.... For if only our own ideas are the objects of our knowledge, how can we possibly know whence those idea arise.... On the other hand, he could be criticised in that, having said that our ideas are the products of the action of the external objects and are copies of such objects, he nevertheless maintained that the substance of objective things is unknowable."*[34]

Moreover, if we further analyse his position it is revealed that Locke in maintaining, that primary qualities are inseparable from their bodies, overlooks the fact that in the process of knowing these qualities we eventually know the material objects. As a result it appears that the status of "material substance" becomes both knowable and unknowable in his ontology.

Thus we infer that the above mentioned inconsistencies in Locke's philosophy arise mainly because of his acceptance of the Cartesian dualism. In this connection it has been commented "*.... The inconsistencies, and contradictions in Locke's epistemology is the outcome of his desire on the* *one hand, to find philosophical foundation of experimental sciences and on the other hand to make room for idealism.*"[35]

In the following section we have shown how Berkeley tries to resolve these inconsistencies by denying dualism and by accepting only the mental side of the Cartesian dualism. In the process he also criticizes Locke's distinction between the primary and secondary qualities. But before that we shall give an account of the "complex ideas" in Locke's epistemology and ontology.

COMPLEX IDEAS

The complex ideas according to Locke, are the universal ideas or the abstract general ideas. These are formed by the various mental operations, e.g., compounding, comparing and abstracting, of the simple ideas. Thus he states "*Combining several simple ideas into one compound one; and thus all complex ideas are made. The second is bringing two ideas, whether simple or complex, together, and setting them by one another, so as to take a view of them at once, without uniting them into one; by which it gets... its ideas of relations. The third is separating them from all other ideas that accompany them in their real existence. This is called abstraction, and thus all its general ideas are made.*"[36] According to Locke the complex ideas so formed are not given in our sensations and reflection. He classifies them under three heads, namely, modes, substances and relations. Explaining the complex idea of Modes, he writes, "*Modes I call such complex ideas which, however, compounded, contain not in them the supposition of subsisting by themselves, but are considered as dependencies on, or affections of substances, such are the ideas signified by the words triangle, gratitude, murder etc.*"[37]

Regarding the complex ideas of substances, he maintains that substances are *"such combinations of simple ideas as are taken to represent distinct particular things subsisting by themselves, in which the supposed idea of substance... is always the first and chief."*[38] He explains the complex idea of substance with the example of man, *"...a combination of the ideas of a certain sort of figure, with the powers of motion, thought, and reasoning, joined to substance, make the ordinary idea of a man."*[39] Thus Locke forms the abstract idea of a man, on the basis of the general or the universal characteristics of a man. We have shown in the next section of that Berkeley rejects the "abstract ideas" of Locke.

Regarding the complex idea of relations, Locke maintains that the idea of relations is formed by the mental operation of "comparing one idea with another". In this context he explains the relation of cause and effect through the concept of "power". He writes, *"Power being the source from whence all action proceeds, the substances wherein these powers are, when they exert this power into act, are called causes, and the substances which there upon are produced or the simple ideas which are introduced into any subject by the exerting of that power are called effects."*[40] For Locke, *"That which produces any simple or complex idea we denote by the general names, cause, and that which is produced, effect."*[41] He asserts that every material substance has some "power" through which one material substance acts on another material substance and brings about `changes' in them. According to him simple ideas are produced out of that 'power' in material substance. We thus find that Locke conceives "cause-effect" relationship among material substance in terms of "power".

A little reflection on the nature of Locke's complex ideas, namely modes, substance and relations, suggest that he uses these complex ideas in his endeavour to explain the external reality within his ontological framework. We have tried to bring out later in the book that both Hume and Ayer deny the existence of Locke's material substance and the relation of cause and effect. They only accept his "modes" in the form of individual "impressions" and "sense-data" respectively.

Having discussed the complex ideas or abstract ideas of material substance and relations of cause and effect, we may now conclude this section by interpreting the subject, object and source of knowledge in Locke. The subject of knowledge, for Locke, appears to us to be the mind as in the case of Descartes, the objects are the true ideas caused by the primary qualities of the material objects and the source is sense-experience.

Locke's position therefore seems to be metaphysical like that of Descartes. Following Descartes, he also takes the subject of knowledge in isolation from its totality. Regarding the source of knowledge he too separates the rational from the empirical, although, as opposed to Descartes he emphasises on the empirical aspect of knowledge. Similarly, in the context of matter, Locke by isolating the primary qualities, separates matter from motion.

With this we now come to the epistemology and ontology of Locke's successor i.e. George Berkeley.

GEORGE BERKELEY (1685-1753)

In this section we have attempted to establish that Berkeley is the first modern empiricist who advocates empiricism in the form of subjective-idealism. He tries to resolve the contradictions which arise in Locke's epistemology by denying the latter's dualism and his concept of abstract ideas. On the other hand, as an empiricist, he accepts only the mental side of Cartesian dualism, and maintains that ideas exist only in the finite and the infinite minds. Thus, his empiricism is of the form of subjective-idealism.

We have endeavoured to show while dealing with Hume's epistemology and ontology, in the ensuing chapter, that although most of his exponents have interpreted him to be a realist, as opposed to those philosophers, he can also be interpreted as a subjective-idealist like Berkeley. Similarly, in the context of Ayer, our aim is to highlight that although his own position, is that he offers an analysis of language, but his analysis itself assumes the presuppositions of Berkeley and Hume. This interpretation is based on the methodological assumption of the distinction between what a philosopher claims to be doing and what he actually does.

Let us now examine Berkeley's epistemology and ontology in order to see his influence on Hume and Ayer..

EPISTEMOLOGY AND ONTOLOGY

In his epistemology, Berkeley strengthens Locke's empiricist premise, namely, that mind can directly know only its ideas But he asserts that these ideas are particular in nature. He does not accept the universal and abstract ideas of Locke. As a result, he denies Locke's complex ideas of substance, modes and relations. In this context while criticising Locke's idea of man as an abstract idea or a universal idea, he writes, "*.... there is no man but* *has some colour, but then it can be neither white, nor black, nor any particular colour, because there is no one particular colour wherein all men partake."*[42] He further writes, *"For myself, I find indeed I have a faculty of imagining or representing to myself, the idea of those particular things I have perceived... the idea of man that I frame to myself must be either of a white, or a black or a tawny, a straight or a crooked, a tall or.... a middle-sized man. I cannot by any effort of thought conceive the abstract idea above described - and it is equally impossible for me to form the abstract idea of motion distinct from body moving...."*[43]

So, Berkeley rejects Locke's universal idea of man. He describes the idea of a man through a combination of the particular qualities or characteristics of an individual. In the process of denying the abstract ideas or the universal ideas, he consequently denies Locke's idea of a material substance which as we have discussed is an abstract idea in his ontology. This results in 'immaterialism'. Hence let us now examine Berkeley's immaterialism.

BERKELEY'S IMMATERIALISM

Berkeley argues that if all we know are the ideas which exist in the mind then there is no justification for asserting any distinction between the ideas of primary and secondary qualities. He argues *"...an idea can be like nothing but another idea; a colour or figure can be like nothing but another colour or figure.... Again, I ask whether those supposed originals or external things, of which our ideas are the pictures or representations, be themselves perceivable or no? If they are, then they are ideas and we have gained our point; but if you say they are not, I appeal to anyone whether it be sense to assert a colour is like something which is invisible; hard or soft, like something which is intangible....*"[44]

He explains his position through the example of an extended body, which, he holds is also coloured, at the same time, "*For my own part, I see evidently that it is not in my power to frame an idea of a body extended and moving, but I must withal give it some colour or other sensible quality which is acknowledge to exist only in the mind. In short, extension, figure, and motion, abstracted from all other qualities, are inconceivable. Where therefore the other sensible qualities are, there must these be also, to wit, in the mind and no where else.* "[45]

He refers to the relativity of the secondary qualities as held by Locke and holds that it is also applicable to the primary qualities. He tries to explain his position with the following example. He says that the same man on boat is said to be stationery in relation to moving stream and again moving in relation to the man standing on the bank.

It accrues, from the above discussion that in Berkeley's ontology, all qualities are mind-dependent. He holds that the primary qualities do not exist externally, but they are ideas which exist in the mind, "*...it is evident... that extension, figure, and motion are only ideas existing in the mind, and that an idea can be like nothing but another idea, and that consequently neither they nor their archetypes can exist in an unperceiving substance. Hence it is plain that the very notion of what is called matter or corporeal substance involves a contradiction in it.*"[46]

It is evident that Berkeley uses the subjectivity of

Locke's secondary quality in order to deny the objectivity of his primary quality. By denying the primary qualities he consequently denies, the material substance of Locke, since according to Locke, as we have already mentioned, primary qualities are inseparable from the material substance. By way of denying the primary qualities as well as the idea of a material substance, he, further denies Locke's causal theory of perception. So in Berkeley's ontology primary qualities and material substance have no objective existence. In this connection he writes in the *Dialogues Between Hylas and Philonous* "*.... if what you mean by the word Matter be only the unknown support of... qualities, it is no matter whether there is such thing or no, since it no way concerns us, and I do not see the advantage there is in disputing about what we know not what, and we know not why.*"[47] Thus Berkeley maintains that all the ideas exist in the mind and are perceived by the mind. "*And to me it is no less evident that the various Sensations, or ideas imprinted in the sense, however blended or combined together (that is, whatever objects they compose), cannot exist otherwise than in a mind perceiving them....*"[48] In this way, we observe that Berkeley strikes a direct chord between the existence of ideas and their being perceived or known by the mind. He explains his position with the example of the table on which he writes, "*The table I write on I say exists that is, I see and feel it, and if I were out of my study I should say it existed - meaning thereby that if I was in my study I might perceive it, or that some other spirit actually does perceive it.... This is all that I can understand by these and the like expressions - for as to what is said of absolute existence of unthinking things without any relation to their being perceived, that is to me perfectly unintelligible. Their* *esse est percipi, nor is it possible they should have any existence out of the minds or thinking things which perceive them.*"[49]

It ensues from the aforementioned lines that Berkeley identifies existence with knowledge unlike Locke, who, as we have shown in the previous section, makes a distinction between existence and knowledge. Criticizing Locke's distinction between knowledge and existence Berkeley maintains that it is based on abstract ideas. While attempting to deny his predecessor's distinction between knowledge and existence, he writes, *"It is indeed an opinion strangely prevailing among men, that houses, mountains... in a word sensible objects, have an existence, natural or real, distinct from their being perceived by the understanding. But... how great an assurance... this principle may be entertained in the world.... For, what are the forementioned objects but the things we perceive by sense? and what do we perceive besides our own ideas and sensations? and is it not plainly repugnant that any of these, or any combination of them, should exist unperceived?"* And he further writes, *"If we thoroughly examine this tenet it will, perhaps, be found at bottom to depend on the doctrine of abstract ideas."*[50]

Thus Berkeley asserts that there is no distinction between the existence of sensible things and our perception of those things. He maintains that sensible things cannot exist without a knowing or perceiving mind. Thus he arrives at his famous dictum of *esse est percipi* i.e., 'to exist is to be perceived'. We shall therefore briefly examine the dictum of *Esse est percipi*.

ESSE EST PERCIPI

Through this dictum Berkeley identifies the objects of knowledge with the source of knowledge. G.E.Moore while criticizing the above dictum of Berkeley's, however, maintains in his "refutation of idealism", that Berkeley's identification of perception with the objects of perception leads him to subjective idealism. (Moore's "refutation of idealism" is briefly discussed in the next chapter.)

Returning to Berkeley, since the source of knowledge, i.e., the "sense-experience" is mind dependent the objects of knowledge also become mind dependent in his ontology. Thus he explains *"Some truths there are so near and obvious to the mind that a man need only open his eyes to see them... in a word all those bodies which compose the mighty frame of the world, have not any subsistence without a mind - that their being is to be perceived or known; that consequently so long as they are not actually perceived by me, or do not exist in my mind or that of any other created spirit, they must either have no existence at all, or else subsist in the mind of some Eternal spirit*"[51]

It follows, that for Berkeley, there is no other substance other than the spiritual substance, which ultimately perceives our ideas. "*...it is evident there is not any other substance than SPIRIT or that which perceives.*"[52] It seems to us that on the basis of the above mentioned dictum of esse est percipe Berkeley assumes the existence of God as the ultimate subject of knowledge in his ontology. For him God is the cause of all our ideas, since he denies the material reality.

But, here a problem arises for Berkeley. It may be

said that the way he denies the idea of a material substance, on the same grounds one may deny the "spiritual" substance. In order to cover up the above mentioned difficulty he holds that we cannot have an idea of God. He maintains that we can have only a `notion' of God. *"We may be said to have some knowledge or notion of our own mind... of spirits... where of in a strict sense we have not ideas."* Thus God appears to be the ultimate "subject" of knowledge for Berkeley. And since the subject of knowledge cannot become the object of knowledge, therefore in his ontology, one cannot have an idea of God but only a "notion" of God.

We have made an effort to show in the coming chapters of the book that following Berkeley's arguments, Hume and Ayer also hold that the subject of knowledge cannot be given in experience. Hence while explaining the subject of knowledge Hume claims it to be a 'bundle of perceptions' and Ayer defines it as a "logical construction out of sense-data".

But even while holding the same position as Berkeley's regarding the subject of knowledge, both Hume and Ayer claim to distinguish between the subject and the object of knowledge. We may admit here that accepting their claims regarding the distinction between the subject and the object of knowledge, many philosophers interpret both these philosophers to be realists. But we have tried to propound during the course of our discussions, that this position is not completely tenable.

It follows from the above account that the nature of reality is mental in the case of Berkeley. Therefore, his position is one of 'subjective idealism'. Commenting on his position it has been said that *"Berkeley's philosophy is designated as subjective-idealism because he maintained that spiritual substance is the only ultimate reality and it is subjective because the objects of knowledge (ideas) depends upon the knowing subject."*[53]

To conclude this section, we have interpreted the three components of knowledge in Berkeley's epistemology and ontology as follows. For him as far as the subject of knowledge is concerned it is the finite or infinite mind thc objects are the particular ideas and the source is sensation. Thus Berkeley also "abstracts" only one aspect of the total concrete reality i.e., the spiritual or mental substance and tries to "absolutise" it. In this manner he follows the footsteps of his predecessors in having a metaphysical attitude.

To sum up, this chapter, I may say that the development of empiricism can be traced from Descartes dualistic assumptions. Whereas through his dualism, he establishes the existence of material substance, Locke, as an empiricist, while attempting to accommodate Descartes dualism, fails to explain the existence of a material substance. Berkeley makes good of Locke's inconsistencies and completely denies the material reality. He accepts only the mental substance. The nature of his reality is therefore mental.

In the next chapter I will show that Hume moves ahead of Berkeley and denies both the mental and the material reality, and asserts the existence of the "impressions" as the only reality.

REFERENCES

1. Suman Gupta, *Twentieth Century Philosophy* (Bangalore, 1991), pp.vi-vii.

2. Suman Gupta, *Man, Science and Social Progress*, ed. by Puchala Satyanarayana (Kakinada, 1995), p. 2.
3. Descartes, *Discourse on Method and the Meditations* translated by F.E. Satcliffe (Penguin Books, 1979), Discourse 4, p. 54.
4. *Ibid.*, p. 53.
5. *Ibid.*, First meditation, p. 96.
6. *Ibid.*, Discourse 4, p. 53.
7. *Ibid.*, p. 54.
8. *Ibid.*, *Second Meditation*, p.103.
9. *Ibid.*, p.105.
10. *Ibid.*
11. *Ibid.*, Discourse 4, p. 54.
12. *Ibid.*, Second Meditation, p. 107.
13. *Ibid.*, p. 105.
14. *Ibid.*, Discourse 4, p. 54.
15. *Ibid.*, p. 55.
16. *Ibid.*, p. 55.
17. *Ibid.*, Sixth Meditation, p.158.
18. *Ibid.*, p. 157.
19. Descartes *Discourse on Method and Meditations*, translated by F.E. Satcliffe (Penguin books 1979) p. 156.
20. Suman Gupta, *Man, Science and Social Progress*, op.cit., p. 3.
21. John Locke, *An Essay Concerning Human Understanding*,

John W. Yolton, Introduction (London, 1976), p.33.

22. *Ibid.*, pp. 33-34.

23. *Ibid.*, p. 34.

24. *Ibid.*, p. 45.

25. *Ibid.*, p. 267.

26. *Ibid.*, p. 45.

27. *Ibid.*, pp. 57-58.

28. *Ibid.*, p. 58.

29. *Ibid.*

30. *Ibid.*, p. 60.

31. *Ibid.*

32. *Ibid.*, p. 60.

33. *Ibid.*, p. 132.

34. Maurice Cornforth, *Science and Idealism* (New York, 1947), p. 32.

35. Suman Gupta, *The Origin and Theories of Linguistic Philosophy* (New Delhi, 1983), p. 43.

36. John Locke, *An Essay Concerning Human Understanding*, op.cit., p.77.

37. *Ibid*, p. 78.

38. *Ibid.*

39. *Ibid.*

40. *Ibid*, p. 130.

41 *Ibid*, p. 155.

42 Berkeley, *The Principles of Human Knowledge*, ed. and introduced by G.J. Warnock (London, 1975), p. 49.

43 *Ibid.*, pp. 49-50.

44. *Ibid.*, p. 68.

45. *Ibid.*, pp. 69-70.

46. *Ibid.*, p. 69.

47. *Ibid.*, p. 103.

48. *Ibid.*, p. 66.

49. *Ibid.*

50. *Ibid.*, pp. 66-67.

51. *Ibid.*, pp. 67-68.

52. *Ibid.*, p. 68.

53. Suman Gupta, *Twentieth Century Philosophy*, p. 33

3

AN EXPOSITION OF THE EPISTEMOLOGY AND ONTOLOGY OF DAVID HUME

After giving an introductory background of the development of British Empiricism, we will now analyse the epistemology and ontology of David Hume (1711-1776). Our main aim in this chapter is to show the unity between Hume's epistemology and ontology. Therefore, for the sake of convenience, we have divided the present chapter into the following basic constituents of his philosophy.

- Hume's empiricism
- Impressions and Ideas
- Denial of the material and the spiritual substance
- Concept of material substance in terms of "laws of association" and "imagination".
- Concept of "self" in relation to "Memory"
- Dichotomy of knowledge between "relations of ideas" and "matters of fact".

We have also endeavoured to show that irresptive of his claims Hume has constantly attempted to defend the commonsense view of the objective material reality and the "self".

Although an analysis of Hume's epistemology and ontology reveals a number of inter-related aspects in his philosophy, for example atomism-pluralism, realism-idealism and so on, we, in this chapter have strived to bring out the realist-idealist controversy in a polemic form, in the context of his theory of Hume's "impressions", as well as his efforts to explain the objective material reality and the self. This is mainly to show how he can also be interpreted as a subjective-idealist philosopher. Since all the above mentioned aspects are closely related with his empiricism, let us first discuss the empiricism of Hume.

HUME'S EMPIRICISM

Hume, in his epistemology, abides by the empiricist premise of both Locke and Berkeley, namely, that the mind can directly know only its ideas, through sense-experience. (The "ideas" of Locke and Berkeley are known as "impressions" in Hume's ontology. we have dealt with his "impressions" in the next section). He agrees with Berkeley, that, if we can directly know only the objects of sensations (which are "impressions" for Hume), then there is no justification for asserting the existence of the material substance. As a result he accepts Berkeley's arguments in order to negate the "abstract ideas" of Locke. These constitute the universal ideas in Locke's ontology, as we have already mentioned in the previous chapter. In this context, while repudiating Locke's abstract ideas or universal idea of man Hume writes, *"The abstract idea of a man represents men of all sizes and all qualities, which it is concluded it cannot do, but either by representing at once all possible sizes and all possible qualities, or by representing no particular one at all. Now, it having been esteemed absurd to defend the former proposition, as implying an infinite capacity in the mind, it has been commonly inferred in favour of the latter; and our abstract ideas have been supposed to represent no particular degree either of quantity or quality. But... this inference is erroneous... it is utterly impossible to conceive any quantity or quality, without forming precise notion of its degrees."*[1] He further writes, *"Abstract ideas are therefore, in themselves individual... The image in the mind is only that of a particular object...."*[2]

Thus Hume declines the Universal ideas of Locke. While supporting Berkeley he also disapproves of Locke's distinction between the ideas of the primary and the secondary qualities (We have discussed this issue in the introductory chapter). In the process of criticising this distinction, he says, *"If colours, sounds, tastes and smells be merely perceptions, nothing we can conceive is possessed of a real, continued and independent existence; not even motion, extension and solidity, which are the primary qualities chiefly insisted on."*[3]

So, for Hume all qualities are nothing but the perceptions in the mind. Consequently, in agreement with Berkeley, he also maintains that there is no distinction between the "primary" and the "secondary" qualities.

We find that so far Hume accepts Berkeley's arguments, in order to deny the material substance of Locke. But he goes a step ahead of Berkeley. He extends Berkeley's criticism of Locke's material substance to his (Berkeley's) mental or spiritual substance, and subsequently denies the mental substance. He argues that the way material substance cannot be given in sense experiences, similarly, even the mental substance cannot be given in sense-experience. Thus Hume renounces both the material and the mental substance. (We have discussed Hume's arguments for the denial of the material and mental substances, in detail, separately in this chapter).

Now the question arises, if there are no material and mental substances, then what, according to Hume, does experience, consist of? In other words, what do we know through sense-experience in his ontology?

According to Hume through sense-experience, we can know only the perceptions. In this context he spells out "*...nothing can be ever presented to the mind, but an image or perception, and... the senses are only inlets through which these images are conveyed, without being able to produce an immediate intercourse between the mind and the object.*"[4] Among these perceptions Hume holds that there are some which are presented to the mind more "forcefully". These are the "lively perceptions" which he calls "impressions". "*...those perceptions which enter with most force and violence, we may name `impressions'*."[5] On the other hand, there are other perceptions which, according to him, are "feeble". These are the "less lively perceptions" and constitute the "ideas" in his philosophy.

It therefore seems that Hume broadly classifies, all sorts of "perceptions" into the above mentioned two kinds, namely "impressions" and "ideas". *"All the perceptions of the human mind resolves themselves into two distinct kinds which I shall call 'impressions' and 'ideas'."*[6] Thus, for him, experience consists only in having the "impressions" and "ideas" without there being neither the material nor the mental substances. In other words "Impressions" and "Ideas", constitute two main categories in his ontology. Hence, we shall now give an exposition of his "impressions" and "ideas".

IMPRESSIONS AND IDEAS

Hume defines an "impression" as, *"By impression then, I mean all our more lively perceptions, when we hear or see or feel or love or hate...."*[7] He also writes regarding impressions, *"...under this name I comprehend all our sensations, passions and emotions as they make their first appearance in the soul."*[8]

So it ensues that for Hume impressions are not only the objects of our sensations, but they also convey our emotions and passions. This aspect is explained by N.K.Smith who writes, *"For the term 'impression' Hume is himself responsible. Employing it as he does, as a term which covers passions, emotions, no less than sensation. Obviously it is not to be interpreted in any etymological sense."*[9]

The "ideas" on the other hand according to him are "faint images" of these "impressions" in our "thinking and reasoning". He writes, *"By ideas, I mean the faint images of these in thinking and reasoning; such as for instance, are all the perceptions excited by the present discourse, excepting only those which arise from the sight and touch, and excepting the immediate pleasure or uneasiness it may occasion.*"[10]

It follows from the above defination of "ideas" that the impressions being the "lively perceptions", are directly given in sense-experience. In fact he identifies impressions with perceptions although he claims that these are a "kind" of our perceptions. He expresses, *"by the term of impressions, I would not be understood to express the manner in which our lively perceptions are produced in the soul, but merely the perceptions themselves; for which there is no particular name, either in the English or any other language that I know of."* "Perceptions" and "impressions" thus have the same connotation in Hume's ontology. He uses the expression "events" in the context of causation, which we have mentioned in the fourth chapter of the book.

On the other hand by restricting ideas only to our "thinking and reasoning", Hume seems to deviate from the Lockean sense of the term "idea". In this context he writes in *Treatise*, *"I here make use of... idea, in a sense different from what is usual.... Perhaps I rather restore the word idea to its original sense, from which Mr. Locke had perverted it, in making it stand for all our perceptions.*"[11]

Since only the impressions are directly given in sense-experience, it seems to us that these "impressions" correspond to the "ideas" of Locke and Berkeley. The identity between Hume's "impressions" and the "ideas" of Locke and Berkeley is pointed out by Suman Gupta. *"All that can exist are what Hume calls impressions. Here we see what Locke and Berkeley call ideas, Hume call impressions.*"[12] It may be mentioned here that what Hume calls "impressions"

(Locke and Berkeley "ideas") are accepted by the linguistic philosophers as "sense-data" or "sense content" (We shall discuss this issue in the third chapter).

Further, in the context of perceptions, he divides all of them into "Simple" and "Complex". He sets forth that every simple idea resembles its corresponding simple impression and similarly every simple impression, its correspondent idea. But according to him, this does not hold "universally true" in the case of "complex impressions and their ideas". *"Simple perceptions, or impressions and ideas, are such as admit of no distinction nor separation. The complex are the contrary to these, and may be distinguished into parts."*[13] However, since the complex impressions are formed out of the simple ones, Hume, in the final analysis contends that both the species of perception, i.e., the "impressions" and "ideas" are correspondent to each other. As a result, it follows that ontologically speaking, these are not two separate categories. The difference between impressions and ideas according to him, consist only in the "degree of force and vivacity". He writes, *"...the first circumstance that strikes my eye, is the great resemblance betwixt our impressions and ideas in every other particular, except their degree of force and vivacity."*[14] It thus follows that for him the difference between the impressions and ideas, is only a difference of degree and not of kind. As a result impressions and ideas both constitute the contents of mind for Hume. *"The one seems to be, in a manner, the reflection of the other; so that all the perceptions of the mind are double, and appear both as impressions and ideas."*

Of the impressions and ideas, he pronounces that we

first have the "simple impressions" from which "simple ideas" are derived later. He thus formulates a "general proposition" in his ontology namely, that *"...all our simple ideas in their first appearance are derived from simple impressions, which are correspondent to them and which they exactly represent."*[15] According to him the impressions are not only connected with the ideas and vice-versa, but the presence of one "influences" the other. *"...that there is a great connection betwixt our correspondent impressions and ideas, and that the existence of the one has a considerable influence upon that of the other."*[16] On the basis of the "constant conjunction" between the impressions and ideas, he concludes that the impressions "precede" the ideas in the order of their "first appearance". He derives from the priority of the impressions that *"our impressions are the causes of our ideas, not our ideas of our impressions."*[17]

We thus find that since Hume denies both the material as well as the mental or spiritual substance, and accepts "impressions" as the only existing reality, therefore, these impressions constitute the causes of the ideas in his ontology. The "impressions" thus form the key concept in Hume's philosophical system. He maintains that there are two kinds of impressions, namely, "impressions of sensation" and "impressions of reflection". The former according to him *"arise in the soul originally from unknown causes", and the latter, "is derived in great measure from our ideas..."*[18]

It is obvious now that ideas have a "secondary" status in his ontology as is implied by the "precedency" of the "impressions". Therefore he declares that all the materials of knowledge are derived from "impressions" alone. *"...all the materials of thinking are derived either from our outward or inward sentiments: the mixture and composition of these belongs alone to the mind.... Or, to express myself in philosophical language, all our ideas or more feeble perceptions are copies of our impressions or more lively ones.*"[19]

Since Hume renounces the category of substance it follows that these impressions exist independently of any support. In the absence of any support they therefore exist "separately" and are thus "distinct" from one another. "*...all our perceptions are different from each other, and from everything else in the universe, they are also distinct and separable, and may be considered as separately existent, and may exist separately and have no need of anything else to support their existence.*"[20] And because all impressions are "distinct" and "separate", it logically follows that Hume's ontological position is a pluralistic one.

Let us now discuss Hume's denial of material substance in more detail. It will be followed by his concept of the material substance.

DENIAL OF THE MATERIAL SUBSTANCE

Hume's denial of substance, logically follows from his pluralist ontology of impressions. As stated earlier according to him only impressions, either of the "sensations" or "reflection", are directly given to us in our sense-experience. He argues that the impressions of "sensations" and "reflection" supply us with specific qualities, not with a unique substratum. To quote, "*If it be perceived by the eyes it must be a colour; if by the ears, a sound; if by the palate, a taste; and so of the other senses. But I believe none will assert, that substance is either of colour, a sound, or a taste. The idea of substance must, therefore, be derived from an impression of reflection, if it really exists. But the impressions of reflection resolve themselves into our passions and emotions; none of which can possibly represent a substance.*"[21] Thus Hume argues that we cannot have an idea of a substance, because according to him a substance is different from an impression or a perception. "*And how can an impression resemble a substance since according to this philosophy, it is not a substance.*"[22]

He further states in the context of material substance, that the "impressions" fail to give us the idea a "continued and distinct existence" which is the characteristic feature of the material substance. Thus he writes, "*...these faculties are incapable of giving rise to the notion of continued existence of their objects.... For that is a contradiction in terms, and supposes that the senses continue to operate, even after they have ceased all manner of operation.*"[23] This is because he reasons out that impressions and ideas are limited to given momentary experience and so cannot justify the existence of external objects. "*They give us no notion of continued existence, because they cannot operate beyond the extent in which they really operate.*"[24] Regarding the "distinct" existence of external material objects, he explains that since these impressions convey us only "single perceptions", there cannot be a distinct existence of the objects. He writes, "*...That our senses offer not their impressions as the images of something distinct... is evident; because they convey to us nothing but a single perception, and never give us the least intimation of anything beyond.*"[25] "*.... They as little produce the opinion of distinct existence, because they neither can offer it... as represented, nor as original. To offer it as represented, they must present both* *our object and image. To make it appear as original, they must convey a falsehood....*"[26] Thus according to Hume we can only form an "opinion" of distinct existence of objects. This is because, he explains that fleeting impressions can neither represent distinct existence nor can they produce them as "originals". As a result he concludes that our senses cannot provide us with ideas of continued and distinct existence of the external objects. "*...We may therefore, conclude with certainty that the opinion of continued and distinct existence never arises from the senses.*"[27] In this way Hume negates the idea of continued and distinct existence of material objects. Since he denies a continued existence he further denies the idea of unperceived existence of objects. This is because, the idea of unperceived existence is contained in the idea of continued existence of material objects. It seems to us that Hume denies both these aspects of reality in order precisely to deny the objective material reality. In this regard it has been commented that *"Hume has rightly pointed out the relationship between `continued existence' and something `independent of perception'. For both objective material reality is the basis. So in order to deny material reality, Hume denied both these aspects of this reality and accepted only the discrete, unrelated, momentary perceptions.*"[28]

Material substance for Hume is therefore, what he calls a "bundle of impressions". Thus, he advocates phenomenalism in his ontology. Phenomenalism, in the context of Hume, implies a position, whereby material substance is reduced to a collection of various impressions. And, by advancing this position, in his ontology he subsequently abolishes the distinction between 'appearance' and `reality'. For him, reality consists of nothing but the "impressions". In this context it has been said that "*The phenomenalists are the empiricists who deny the distinction between appearance and reality. They hold that only what is "given in experience" can exist.*"[29]

We have tried to show in the succeeding section that Hume's analysis of the mental substance or the self also brings to light his phenomenalism. And in the following chapter we have focussed on the issue that the phenomenalist interpretation of the material objects and the 'self' holds valid in Ayer's ontological framework too. In other words we have ventured to bring out that following Hume, Ayer also abolishes the distinction between appearance and reality.

But a problem arises for Hume. We know that in the external reality material objects do exist even when they are not perceived by us. How does Hume explain this common-sense view of an unperceived existence of the objects which constitute the external material reality?

While attempting to interpret the material objects, Hume uses the category of "ideas" in his ontology. He explains his position through the examples of tables and houses, and writes, "*The table which we see, seems to diminish, as we remove farther from it; but the real table, which exists independently of us suffers no alternation... the existences, which we consider, when we say, this house and that tree, are... nothing but... fleeting copies or representations of other existences which remains uniform and independent.*"[30] "Copies or representations" in the above statement are nothing but ideas of Hume, which follows from his definition of the term "idea" as we have already seen.

Now, it may also be asked that if material substance is nothing but "bundle of impressions", how does Hume explain the 'concrete' material objects which exist in the reality.

In order to to explain the existence of the concrete material objects, Hume introduces "laws of association" in his ontology. He asserts that the laws of association, unite the several, discrete and unconnected impressions, because of which these impressions appear as inseparably connected in the "imagination" and in our "memory" they appear as "united". (We have discussed the concept of "memory" separately in the following section, in the context of Hume's concept of the self.) The "inseparable connection" among the impressions is therefore, only apparent. In fact he maintains that there is only a "gentle force" of attraction among the various impressions, which "associates" the various impressions together. This association arises from the "qualities" of "resemblance", "contiguity" in time and place, and "cause and effect", among the various fleeting impressions. These three qualities which are also the "relations" among the impressions, constitute the "uniting principle" or the "laws of association" in Hume's ontology. He explains these laws through "imagination" because according to him, all simple ideas and impressions are united by the faculty of imagination. Hence let us now state these laws and see how Hume uses the faculty of "imagination" in constructing the material objects.

LAWS OF ASSOCIATION AND THE ROLE OF IMAGINATION IN HUME'S ONTOLOGY

Hume maintains that the relation of resemblance is "fundamental" to all relations. This is because, according to him, in the absence of this relation, there can be no comparison among the various objects. He writes, "*...and this is a relation, without which no philosophical relation can exist, since no objects will admit of comparison, but what have some degree of resemblance.*"[31]

On the basis of the resemblance among objects (which are Hume's impressions), he claims to ascribe an "identity" to the material objects. He describes identity as one of the "most universal relations" since according to him identity renders "unchangeability" to the objects. "*Identity may be esteemed a second species of relation. This relation I here consider as applied in its strictest sense to constant and unchangeable objects....*"[32]

Regarding the relation of "contiguity" he writes, "*After identity the most universal and comprehensive relations are those of space and time, which are the sources of an infinite number of comparisons such as distant, contiguous, above, below, before, after, etc.*"[33] It is implied from the above statement that the relation of contiguity, brings the various objects together.

Similarly, Hume maintains that the relation of "cause and effect" among the various impressions also give rise to the idea of continued existence of the material objects. He says that because of this relation among the objects, the mind, on the basis of the repeated occurrence of an event in the past, "expects" it to occur, through its own `imagination' in the future also. The relation of cause and effect, according to him thus produces a "customary transition" in the mind, as a result of which, the mind "believes" in the continued existence of the external material substance. (This aspect of hume's philosophy has been dealt in the fourth chapter.)

Finally, in the context of "imagination" he writes, *"Nothing is more free than the imagination of man; and though it cannot exceed that original stock of ideas furnished by the internal and external senses, it has the unlimited power of mixing, compounding, separating and dividing these ideas in all the varieties... of vision."*[34] It follows that the imagination has the capacity to associate or dissociate the various impressions and their ideas. Since imagination has "unlimited power" to unite our distinct impressions and perceptions, through the laws of association, therefore, it seems to us that imagination plays a significant role in the construction of material objects. The role of imagination as well as that of the laws of association is explained by Hume in the following words. *"It is plain, that in the course of our thinking, and in the constant revolution of our ideas, our imagination runs easily from one idea to any other that resembles it, and that this quality alone is to the fancy a sufficient bond and association. It is likewise evident, that as the senses, in changing their objects, are necessitated to change them regularly, and take them as they lie contiguous to each other, the imagination must by long custom acquire the same method of thinking, and run along the parts of space and time in conceiving its objects. As to the connection that is made by the relation of cause and effect.... it is sufficient to observe, that there is no relation, which produces a stronger connection in the fancy, and makes one idea more readily recall another, than the relation of cause and effect betwixt their objects."*[35] On the basis of the analysis of the above mentioned laws of association, it appears that continued existence. of an object within Hume's ontological framework occurs only in the mind or our thoughts. It is therefore `subjective' and does not have any relevance with the objective world. In this context Hume himself writes, "*these are the uniting principles in the ideal world and without them every distinct object is separated by the mind*."[36] Thus he explains the continued and uninterrupted existence of the particular material objects in the external reality, with his "laws of association" and the concept of "imagination".

Besides the above mentioned laws of association, he also uses the concept of "coherence" and "constancy" in order to explain the `concrete' and continued existence of the material objects.

Regarding "constancy", he writes "*...all those objects, to which we attribute a continued existence, have a peculiar constancy, which distinguishes them from the impressions whose existence depends upon our perceptions*."[37] Similarly, in the context of "coherence" he writes, "*Bodies often change their position and qualities.... But here it is observable, that even in these changes they preserve a coherence, and have a regular dependence on each other; which is the foundation of a kind of reasoning from causation, and produces the opinion of their continued existence*."[38]

Let us now examine Hume's denial of the mental substance or the 'self'.

HUME'S DENIAL OF THE SELF

Hume's denial of the self results from the same arguments that he uses in order to reject the idea of the material substance. He argues that we cannot have an idea of the mental substance or the 'self' since the 'self' cannot be given in sense-experience. In other words he claims that there is no idea of a 'self' since there are no impressions corresponding to this idea of a 'self'. He thus denounces the existence of the self which forms the spiritual substance in Berkeley's ontology. To this effect he writes, "*When we talk of self or substance, we must have an idea annexed to these terms otherwise they are altogether unintelligible. Every idea is derived from preceding impressions; and we have no impression of self or substance, as something simple and individual. We have, therefore, no idea of them in that sense.*"[39]

It follows, that for Hume, there can be no idea of a "self" apart from an "impression" of the "self". To quote, "*... from what impression could this idea be derived? This question it is impossible to answer without a manifest contradiction and absurdity; .... It must be some one impression that gives rise to every real idea. But self or person is not any one impression, but that to which our several impressions and ideas are supposed to have a reference. If any impression gives rise to the idea of self, that impression must continue invariably the same, through the whole course of our lives; since self is supposed to exist after that manner. But there is no impression constant and invariable.' Pain and pleasure,... passions and sensations succeed each other, and never all exist at the same time. It cannot therefore be from any of these impressions, or from any other, that the idea of self is derived, and consequently there is no such idea.*"[40]

Here again Hume faces a difficulty. Our experience tells us that we do have a "self" of which we are every moment conscious. So, how does Hume explain this consciousness of self if there is no idea of self? Hume avows that the assumption of the self is based on the connection which appears among the various perceptions or impressions and ideas. He writes, "*...For my part, when I enter most intimately into what I call myself I always stumble on some particular perception or other, of heat or cold, light or shade, love or hatred, pain or pleasure. I never can catch myself, at any time without a perception, and never can observe anything but the perception.*"[41] Thus he attempts to explain away the self, on the basis of a composition of our various perceptions. The self, in his ontology, is therefore nothing but a collection of different perceptions. "*...I may...affirm of the rest of mankind, that they are nothing but a bundle or collection of different perceptions, which succeed in each other with an inconceivable rapidity, and are in a perpetual flux and movement.*"[42] So the entire mankind is reduced to to a "bundle of various perceptions". It is thus found that there is a phenomenalistic assumption behind Hume's analysis of the self.

Since, the perceptions, which according to him, compose the self, are variable and successive in nature, he consequently denies the idea of a "personal identity" among the various perceptions of the self. According to him the idea of "personal identity" occurs only in our "thoughts" and "imagination". Thus he writes, "*What then gives us so great a propension to ascribe an identity to these successive perceptions, and to suppose ourselves possessed of an invariable and uninterrupted existence through the whole course of our lives? In order to answer this question we must distinguish betwixt personal identity, as it regards our thought or imagination, and as it regards our passions.... The first is our present subject.*"[43] It ensues from the above statement that for Hume the identity among the various perceptions is produced by the imagination. "*...that identity is nothing really belonging to these different perceptions, and uniting them together, but is merely a quality which we attribute to them, because of the union of their ideas in the imagination when we reflect upon them.*"[44] In this context he further asserts , "*...we often feign some new and unintelligible principle, that connects the objects together, and prevents their interruption or variation.*"[45]

So, it is apparent that Hume uses the faculty of "imagination" to explicate the continued existence of material substance as well as the "personal identity" of "self". The continued existence of the self in Hume's ontology, is thus not real. It is only fictitious. He ferrets out, in this context, "*Thus we feign the continued existence of the perceptions of our senses, to remove the interruption; and run into the notion of a soul, and self, and substance, to disguise the variation.*"[46] It is thus derived that one cannot justify an identity of the self within Hume's ontological framework. "*...we feel a propensity to confound these ideas, though we are not able fully to satisfy ourselves in that particular, nor find anything invariable and uninterrupted to justify our notion of identity.* "[47]

In this way it is observed that Hume repudiates the notion of a "personal identity", among the several "distinct" perceptions of the self. "*It is evident, that the identity which we attribute to the human mind, however perfect we may imagine it to be, is not able to run the several different perceptions into one, and make them lose their characters of distinction and difference, which are essential to them. It is still true that every distinct perception which enters into the composition of the mind, is a distinct existence, and is different and distinguishable, and separable from every other perception, either contemporary or successive.*"[48]

The above discussion manifests that within Hume's ontological framework the idea of a "personal identity" of the "self" is only `subjective' and has no objective significance. But if we look at the self, from a common sense point of view, we do observe some real bond among our various perceptions or that of other people, due to which we not only ascribe an identity to ourselves but also to others. How does Hume explain this common-sense position.?

Hume endeavours to explain the common-sense view of personal identity on the basis of the relations of "resemblance" and "causation" and in this context he explains causation with the help of the concept of "memory". Thus whereas he introduces "imagination" in his attempt to explain the material reality, he introduces the concept of "memory" while attempting to explain the "personal identity" of the self.

CONCEPT OF SELF IN RELATION TO MEMORY

While explaining the role of "memory" and "resemblance", he maintains that the `memory', on the basis of the relation of "resemblance", among the perceptions make the mind believe in the "appeared personal identity" of the self. He writes, "*To begin with resemblance; suppose we could see clearly into the breast of another, and observe that succession of perceptions which constitutes his mind or thinking principle, and suppose that he always preserves the memory of a considerable part of past perceptions, it is evident that nothing could more contribute to the bestowing a relation on this succession amidst all its variations. For what is the memory but a faculty by which we raise up the images of past perceptions? And as an image necessarily resembles its object, must not the frequent placing of these resembling perceptions in the chain of thought, ...make the whole seem like the continuance of one object? In this particular, then the memory not only discovers the identity, but also contributes to its production, by producing the relation of resemblance among the perceptions. The case is the same, whether we consider ourselves or others."*[49]

In a similar strain, while expatiating the role of the law of causation in the context of "self", Hume holds that the relation of cause and effect, links together the various perceptions of the mind. As a result he claims that our memory conveys that they have continued existence. "*As to causation; we may observe that the true idea of the human mind, is to consider it as a system of different perceptions or different existences, which are linked together by the relation of cause and effect, and mutually produce, destroy, influence, and modify each other. Our impressions give rise to their correspondent ideas; and these ideas, in their turn produce other impressions. One thought chases another, and draws after it a third, by which it is expelled in its turn."*[50] He further writes, "*As memory alone acquaints us with the continuance and extent of this succession of perceptions, it is to be considered, upon that account chiefly as the source of personal identity. Had we no memory, we never should have any notion of causation, nor consequently of that chain of causes and effects, which constitute self or person.*"[51] So Hume explains away the notion of self through the human faculty of memory.

But at the same time he also maintains that our 'memory' cannot remember all the perceptions and incidents of past. He raises a doubt, *"For how few of our past actions are there, of which we have any memory?"*[52] And in the final analysis he concludes, "In this view, *therefore, memory does not so much produce as discover personal identity, by showing us the relation of cause and effect among our different perceptions.*"[53]

It follows according to Hume that our memory induces the relation of cause and effect which in turn ascribes an "identity" to the self. It is also implied that our 'memory' ascribes forgotten events to the self through the relation of causation. There is thus a fallacy in Hume's philosophy while he attempts to explain the idea of the "self" through the relation of causation and the concept of "memory". On the one hand he claims that had there been no memory, we would not have any idea of causation, and on the other hand he holds that memory cannot remember all the perceptions of the past and so it is the relation of cause and effect which unites the forgotten incidents, and ascribes an identity to the self. This is a logical fallacy in Hume's analysis of the appeared identity of the self.

Having established Hume's overall pluralist- empiricist position which logically follows from his denial of the mental and material substance, let us now examine whether Hume is a realist or a subjective-idealist. On this account Hume's exponents can be categorised into two classes. Some interpret him as a realist and others as idealist. We shall first mention the realist position and then state the subjective-idealist interpretation.

Hume has been widely interpreted as a realist, because of his denial of the mental substance. Since, he asserts that the impressions exist independently of mind, it is maintained by most of his exponents that the impressions are objective. As a result, Hume is regarded as a realist by these philosophers. The realist position may be briefly explained, through Moore's "refutation of idealism". Through this article, Moore refutes Berkeley's dictum of *esse est percipi* and consequently, his identification of the objects of sensations with sensations.

Moore argues that object of sensation and sensation are not identical because for example, when we perceive 'blue', it is not a sensation of 'blue', it is awareness of blue as an object. In other words to be "aware of blue" is not to have in the minds a representative image of which blue is the part of the object. He points out that *esse est percipi* is seen to be false as soon as it is seen that *esse* (to exist) and *percipi* (to be perceived) are two distinct terms like "green" and "sweet" which cannot be necessarily related together. In order to explain his position, he takes the example of the sensation of blue and sensation of green. He maintains that there is a difference only in respect of the objects (blue and green) of sensation and not in respect of sensation which is a form of consciousness common to both. He explains that every sensation comprises of two distinct elements namely,

(i) Consciousness in respect of which all sensations are alike.

(ii) Something else, the object, in respect of which one sensation differs from another.

Thus he asserts that it is wrong to identify the object with the consciousness of it. In this way he refutes Berkeley's idealist contention. According to him an idealist says that blue is the same thing as sensation, he identifies one part of a complex whole (namely "sensation of blue") with another part which is distinct from the first. But if he says *that blue is the same thing as the sensation of blue, he identifies a part with the whole. In both cases, Moore expresses that the idealist is absurd. For him and for the realists existence of objects is very distinct from the knowledge of it*"[54]

In agreement with the realist position, Jonathan Dancy interprets Hume to be a realist. According to Dancy, for Hume impression is the only reality which can exist independently of the mind. In other words, *he maintains that Hume emphasizes on facts which can be known independently of anything. Thus Dancy argues that Hume is a realist.*"[55]

Hume has also been interpreted as a realist on the basis of his explanation of continued existence of external material reality. Interpreting him to be a realist on these grounds, Gallen Strawson writes, *"My purpose, here is to merely support those philosophers in the belief that it makes senses to suppose that there is truth of the matter here... the realist thought of reality is indeed real and it does indeed have a certain nature whatever we can or cannot know about it.*"[56]

Besides, Strawson we find that Daniel E.Flage, also

interprets Hume to be a realist in his book, *David Hume's Theory of Mind*. He refers to Hume's use of the concepts of coherence and constancy to explain the material reality and holds that he advocates direct realism. He writes, *"Asking what Hume's views were regarding the problem of perception and existence of the external world, I argue that he favoured a form of direct realism, taking external world to be what ever it is that is described by the laws of Newtonian mechanics and causes one's `impressions'. This is suggested by Hume's discussion of constancy and coherence."*[57]

Similarly, John Bricke interprets Hume to be a realist on the basis of his explanation of "self-identity". Brick maintains that Hume's account of 'self-identity' and the theory of `self' is very much satisfactory. He claims *that a subjective idealist cannot provide such satisfactory analysis of the "self" therefore for him Hume is not a subjective idealist. And in his concluding remarks he says that Hume is a realist. "If Hume were a subjective idealist he could not provide a satisfactory account of self identity based on causality. At least, he could not do so without giving up fundamental elements in his theories of causality and of the mind. For the crux of my present objection is Hume's need to provide for causal continuity. I do not see how, if he were a subjective idealist, Hume could manage this."*[58]

The above mentioned realist interpretation is however not tenable. This is because there are other philosophers who precisely on the basis of Berkeley's *esse est percipi* maintain that the sensations cannot be abstracted from the person who has these sensations. These are the subjective-idealist philosophers who disagree with Moore's realist interpretation. In support of this interpretation Suman Gupta writes: *"All that existed for Hume are the impressions and ideas which are the only entities given in sense-experience. Logically impressions and ideas cannot have an ontological status without existing in some kind of a mind however abstract it may be. This is the reason we regard Hume's position to be empiricist subjective idealist."*[59] According to this interpretation, the impressions of Hume are mental and subjective. Suman Gupta further writes, *"Ontologically speaking these impressions, for Hume, are transitory, mental, discrete, unconnected subjective elements out of which the whole mental and material world is constituted."*[60] Thus, as opposed to the realist claim, the subjective-idealist philosophers assert that for Hume, like Berkeley there is no distinction between impressions and the sensations of impressions.

Contrary to Strawson and Daniel Flage's realist interpretation of Hume, it seems to us on the basis of methodology we have adopted that language, ontology and epistemology are all interrelated aspects of the objective material reality. So Hume's explanation of the external material reality or his concept of material substance, may be interpreted as a consequence of his 'linguistic compulsion'. We may here refer to Suman Gupta who writes, *"Hume... constantly assumed the existence of the material world although his aim was to deny it. This is bound to be the case because our language, which Hume also had to use, is meant to communicate a real world and not the distorted world view of the idealist philosopher. No communication among human beings is possible without assuring human beings, their surrounding world, their practical activity....*

Hume wanted to communicate his idealist world-view through a language which he logically cannot do. Consequently he assumed everything which he wanted to deny."[61]

Suman Gupta maintains that the language used by Hume communicates an 'abstract' reality which consists of only the impressions, all of which are 'abstracted from their material reality'. While attempting to show that Hume already assumes a material substance, she quotes him, in her book *The Origin and Theories of Linguistic Philosophy* and writes, "*the several distinct ideas of colour, which enter by the eye,... are really different from each other; though, at the same time resembling. Now if this be true of colours, it must be no less so of the different shades of the same colour*."[62] Suman Gupta claims "*we may note here that Hume cannot without committing a contradiction, talk of 'eyes' and 'ears' which are physical organs of the body when he denies the existence of material reality.*"[63] Thus according to Suman Gupta, Hume already assumes a material reality. This is because without this assumption, mere coherence and constancy cannot give us any idea of the external world.

The above interpretation is supported by E.E.Harris when he says, "*constancy and coherence would then have disintegrated and imaginative construction of an external world would have been revealed as sheer fantasy... for if our impressions are nothing but particulars and all `ideas' are nothing but copies of them, no imaginative construction could be made*."[64] Thus on the basis of Flage's arguments we cannot interpret Hume to be a realist. So we find that the realist interpretation of Hume is not completely tenable.

Coming to Hume's explanation of "self" through the

concept of "memory" we find that like the continued existence of the material substance, the idea of "personal identity" of the "self" has no objective significance in his ontological framework. This subjectivity in Hume is also brought about by George Novack. Novack writes, *"Hume shifted whole weight of knowledge on the subjective side. However, the solitary self is too weak to sustain so great a burden. Actually, if Hume's contentions were true, the entire structure of human knowledge collapse for the lack of support of objective reality."*[65]

As we have already stated in the introduction, the denial of the category of substance is inseparably linked with a philosopher's analysis of knowledge. Since Hume denies the category of substance, we find that there is no certain knowledge for him. On the other hand he claims that our knowledge of the 'matters of fact' is only a probable knowledge. He relates "matters of fact" to "probability" by using verification as a 'criterion of truth'. For him, only knowledge of the "impressions" are true, as these are the only entities which are 'verifiable' through our sense-experience. To this effect he writes, *"All knowledge revolves itself into probability and becomes at last of the same nature with that evidence, which we employ in common life."*[66]

We have tried to show in the next chapter that this interpretation holds good in the case of Ayer also. However, we do have certain and universal knowledge like that of mathematics and logic. Hence a question arises: how does Hume in his ontological framework account for such knowledge?

In his attempt to accommodate certain and universal knowledge, Hume in his epistemology, makes a division of all knowledge between "relations of ideas" and "matters of fact". The "matters of fact" constitute what we have already discussed. The "relations of ideas" on the other hand comprise of knowledge of mathematics, logic and so on. Thus Hume writes in the *Enquiries*, *"All the objects of human reason or enquiry may naturally be divided into two kinds, to wit, Relations of Ideas, and Matters of Fact. Of the first kind are the sciences of Geometry, Algebra, and Arithmetic; and in short, every affirmation which is either intuitively or demonstratively certain.... Propositions of this kind are discoverable by the mere operation of thought, without dependence on what is anywhere existent in the universe....*

Matters of fact, which are the second objects of human reason, are not ascertained in the same manner; nor is our evidence of their truth, however great, of a like nature with the foregoing. The contrary of every matter of fact is still possible; because it can never imply a contradiction, and is conceivable by the mind with the same facility and distinctness, as if ever so conformable to reality. That the sun will not rise tomorrow is no less intelligible a proposition, and implies no more contradiction than the affirmation, that it will rise. We should in vain, therefore, attempt to demonstrate its falsehood. Were it demonstratively false, it would imply a contradiction, and could never be distinctly conceived by the minds."[67]

It is evident that Hume tries to explain certain and universal knowledge through intuition alone, without any reference to the empirical facts. and in doing so he thus separates the rational aspect of knowledge from its empirical aspect. Hume's dichotomy of knowledge is also reflected in the context of Ayer's classification of meaningful propositions into analytic and synthetic propositions. We have deliberated on this issue in the next chapter.

On the basis of Hume's division of knowledge between "relations of ideas" and "matters of fact" it follows that he exhausts all knowledge between these two categories. And any knowledge which does not fall between these categories, he claims it to be "metaphysical". Thus he tries to get rid of metaphysics from the realm of philosophy on the basis of his dichotomy of knowledge. Hume's opposition to metaphysics is evident when he writes, *"when we run over libraries, persuaded of these principles, what havoc must we make? If we take in our hand any volume; of divinity or school metaphysics, for instance; let us ask, does it contain any abstract reasoning concerning matter of fact and existence? No. Commit it then to the flames; for it can contain nothing but sophistry and illusion."*[68] Thus Hume claims to eliminate metaphysics.

We would like to mention here that the concept metaphysics is used by Hume in the sense of supersensible reality. We have discussed the other senses of the concept of metaphysics in the next chapter. To sum up the present chapter we may say that by denying the material substance, Hume consequently denies the object of knowledge. And his denial of the mental substance or the self entails his subsequent denial of the subject of knowledge. In the absence of a concrete subject and object of knowledge, *i.e.,* a mental and material reality, respectively, Hume's 'impressions' and perceptions as well his sensations as the source of knowledge, are nothing but 'mental' abstractions. It therefore appears that although he denies the mental substance, his assertion that "impressions" are the only reality imply that he assumes Descartes' mental side of the Cartesian dualism. His approach therefore appears to be metaphysical like that of his predecessors. (We have stated this sense of the term 'metaphysical' in the context of Descartes, Locke and Berkeley and also in the third chapter.)

The abstract fragmentary perceptions cannot give the idea of a 'unitary self' within Hume's ontological framework. But a scientific or a common-sense analysis of knowledge do presuppose a concrete subject of knowledge as well as the dialectical interaction between the subject and objects of knowledge. Since Hume's objects of knowledge are equally fragmentary consequently, he claims to deny certain universal and necessary knowledge of the "matters of fact". His emphasis on the empirical aspect of knowledge makes him a-scientific. This is because, a scientific analysis of knowledge includes both the rational and the empirical aspects in the conceptual apparatus of knowledge.

In the ensuing chapter of this book, we have made an affort to unravel the ontological and epistemological aspects of Ayer's linguistic philosophy. Our attempt is to show that it can be traced from Hume's philosophy, which we have discussed in this chapter.

REFERENCES

1. David Hume, *A Treatise of Human Nature*, Book I, edited by D.G.C.Macnabb (Glasgow,1978), pp. 61-62.

2. *Ibid.,* p. 64.

3. *Ibid.*, p. 278.

4. David Hume, *Enquiries* (ed.) L.A.Selby-Bigge, 3rd edition (Oxford, 1976), p. 152.
5. David Hume, *A Treatise of Human Nature, op.cit.,* p. 45.
6. *Ibid.*
7. David Hume, *Enquiries, op.cit.,* p. 18.
8. David Hume, *Treatise*, op.cit., p. 45.
9. N.K.Smith, *The Philosophy of David Hume: A Critical Study of Its Origins and Central Doctrines* (London, 1941), p. 15.
10. David Hume, *Treatise, op.cit.,* p. 45.
11. *Ibid*, p. 46
12. Suman Gupta, "Bertrand Russell and A.J.Ayer: A Dialectico-Materialist Approach", *Marxian Sociology*, vol.2, 1979, p. 298.
13. David Hume, *Treatise*, op.cit., p. 46.
14. *Ibid.*
15. *Ibid*, p. 48.
16. *Ibid.*
17. *Ibid,* p. 49.
18. *Ibid*, p. 51.
19. David Hume, *Enquiries, op.cit.,* p. 19.
20. David Hume, *Treatise, op. cit.,* pp. 283-284.
21. *Ibid*, pp. 59-60.
22. *Ibid*, p. 283.
23. *Ibid,* p. 239.

24. *Ibid*, p. 242.

25. *Ibid,* p. 240.

26. *Ibid*, pp. 242-243.

27. *Ibid*, p. 243.

28. Suman Gupta, *op.cit.,* p. 67.

29. Suman Gupta, "A.J.Ayer: A Loss to the World of Philosophy", p. 302.

30. David Hume, *Enquiries*, *op.cit.,* p. 152.

31. David Hume, *Treatise*, *op.cit.*, p. 58.

32. *Ibid.*

33. *Ibid.*

34. David Hume, *Enquiries*, *op.cit.,* p. 47.

35. David Hume, *Treatise*, *op.cit.*, p. 55.

36. David Hume, *Treatise*, Ernest C.Mossner (ed.) (Baltimore, 1969), pp.307-8.

37. David Hume, *Treatise*, *op.cit.*, p. 245.

38. *Ibid.*, p. 246.

39. *Ibid.,* p. 328.

40. *Ibid.*, p. 301.

41. *Ibid.,* pp. 301-2.

42. *Ibid.*, p. 302.

43. *Ibid.*, p. 303.

44. *Ibid.*, p. 309.

45. *Ibid.*, p. 304.

46. *Ibid.*, p. 304.

47. *Ibid.*

48. *Ibid.*, p. 309.

49. *Ibid.*, p. 310.

50. *Ibid.*

51. *Ibid.*, p. 311.

52. *Ibid.*

53. *Ibid.*, p. 312.

54. G.E.Moore in *Mind*, quoted by D.M.Datta, *The Chief Currents of Contemporary Philosophy* (Patna, 1972), pp. 301-5.

55. Jonathan Dancy, *Berkeley: An Introduction* (New York, 1987), p. 11.

56. Gallen Strawson, *The Secret Connection: Causation, Realism and David Hume* (Oxford, 1989), p. 61.

57. Daniel E.Flage, *David Hume's Theory of Mind* (London, 1990), p. 126.

58. John Bricke, *David Hume: Bicentenary Papers*, G.P.Morice (ed.) (Edinburgh, 1977), p. 173.

59. Suman Gupta, *The Critique of Wittgenstein* (New Delhi, 1986), p. 25.

60. Suman Gupta, *Origin and Theories of Linguistic Philosophy*, *op.cit.*, p. 64.

61. *Ibid*, p. 69.

62. David Hume, *Enquiries*, quoted by Suman Gupta, *op.cit.*, p. 66.

63. *Ibid.*

64. E.E.Harris, *Nature, Mind and Modern Science* (New York), p. 180.

65. George Novack, *Empiricism and Its Revolution: A Marxist Point of View* New York,1973), pp.68-69.

66. David Hume, *Treatise*, *op.cit.*, p. 232.

67. David Hume, *Enquiries*, *op.cit.*, pp. 25-26.

68. David Hume *An Enquiry concerning Human Understanding* in A.J. Ayer and R. Winch ed *British Empirical Philosophers* (New York 1968), p. 515.

4

AN EXPOSITION OF THE EPISTEMOLOGY AND ONTOLOGY OF A.J. AYER

Having analysed the epistemological and ontological positions of Hume in the previous chapter, we will now proceed to examine the epistemology.and ontology of A.J. Ayer (1910-1989). We have strived to show that it can be traced from Hume's epistemology and ontology. In order to achieve the afforesaid objectives, it is necessary to mention Ayer's basic philosophical claims regarding the subject-matter, method and aim of philosophy.

It seems that Ayer confines the subject matter of philosophy to language, using analysis as the only method of philosophy, and the aim of philosophy according to him consists in the clarification of concepts and propositions of ordinary language and science.

Contrary to his above mentioned claims, namely, that the method and consequently subject-matter of philosophy consists of a "neutral" analysis of language, we have tried to show in this chapter, that his analysis assumes certain ontological presuppositions, which are similar to Hume's ontological presuppositions. On the basis of these ontological presuppositions we have attempted to bring out that he subsequently arrives at an epistemology which resembles Hume's epistemology. This is because a philosopher's views on language and meaning are logically bound up with his world-view *i.e.,* a particular ontology and epistemology. *"No philosophy can be pure analysis of linguistic concepts. All philosophies whether openly or in a disguised form contain a world-view and the world-view of a specific philosophy is conditioned by the objective reality."*[1]

As in the earlier chapters , here too, we have attempted to unravel the ontological and epistemological aspects of Ayer's linguistic-philosophy in terms of what a philosopher claims to be doing and what he actually does. His legacy to Hume is evident from his own remarks when he writes in *Language, Truth and Logic "The views which are put forward in this treatise... are... the logical outcome of the empiricism of... David Hume."*[2] He redoubles this claim in *Logical Positivism in Perspective*, *"Apart from my later works, I sometimes think of Language, Truth and Logic itself as being no more than Hume in modern dress."*[3]

In order to trace the ontological premises of Ayer, we have divided his philosophy, for the sake of convenience, into the following aspects:

1. Classification of propositions into analytic and synthetic.
2. Verification principle.

3. Sense-contents.
4. Denial of the material substance and 'self'.
5. Phenomenalism.
6. Denial of a supersensible reality and also the denial of an 'objective material reality'.

We have discussed these aspects in terms of their inter-relations and inter-dependence and have attempted to show that they are a re-statement of Hume's ontological aspects, but for Ayer's use of a 'linguistic make up'.

Let us now discuss the classification of the analytic and synthetic propositions.

ANALYTIC AND SYNTHETIC PROPOSITIONS

As has been already stated in the last chapter, Hume divides all knowledge between "Relations of ideas" and "Matters of fact". Following Hume's epistemological dichotomy, Ayer, in his semantic framework classifies all meaningful propositions between 'analytic' and 'synthetic' propositions. He makes this distinction in order to reject Mill's view that analytic propositions have the same status as empirical hypotheses. Mill maintains that the truths of logic and mathematics which constitutes Ayer's analytic propositions, are not necessary or certain. He considers these propositions to be inductive generalizations, which are based on an extremely large number of instances. As a result, he avows that these generalizations can be easily confuted. So *he concludes that the propositions of mathematics and logic are "probable" like the empirical hypotheses, but they are not certain.*"[4]

Contrary to Mill, Ayer proposes that the validity of analytic propositions, "depends solely on the definitions of the symbols it contains."[5] He expatiates that the truths of logic and mathematics which are analytic propositions are tautologous because, "*...they are independent of experience in the sense that they do not owe their validity to empirical verification.*"[6] Thus as opposed to Mill, he asserts that all logical and mathematical propositions are "necessarily true". In this context he writes, "*...once we have apprehended them we see that they are necessarily true, that they hold good for every conceivable instance.*"[7] Regarding the synthetic propositions, Ayer on the other hand, maintains that these propositions are dependent on sense experience. He writes, "*a proposition is... synthetic when its validity is determined by the facts of experience.*"[8] These propositions, according to him, are not universal and necessary. "*...a proposition whose validity depends upon experience cannot be seen to be necessarily and universally true.*"[9] As a result, he concludes that the synthetic propositions are highly "probable". The nature of Ayer's 'analytic" and 'synthetic' propositions are therefore similar to that of Hume's "relations of ideas" and "matters of fact" respectively, which we have already discussed in the last chapter. It therefore follows that Ayer converts Hume's epistemological division of the "relations of ideas" and "matters of fact" into a semantic one.

It may be asked how does Ayer relate the probability of the synthetic propositions to sense-experience? In his attempt to answer this question, he claims to use the "criterion of verification". We have stated in the context of Hume that he uses verification as a 'criterion of truth'. Ayer on the other hand, uses it as a criterion of "meaning" in terms of his semantic framework. He thus identifies knowledge as equivalent to the analysis of the concept of knowledge.

Hence let us now discuss the verification principle of meaning in order to see how he relates the synthetic proposition with the sense experiences and declares them as 'probable'.

VERIFICATION PRINCIPLE OF MEANING

Ayer defines the verification principle of meaning as, *"a criterion by which it can be determined whether or not a sentence is literally meaningful. A simple way to formulate it would be to say that a sentence had literal meaning if and only if the proposition it expressed was either analytic or empirically verifiable."*[10] Since the analytic propositions are independent of experience and already constitute the necessary truths, therefore, it logically follows that the principle of verifiability, as a criterion of "literal meaning" or "literal significance" is applicable only to his "synthetic" propositions.

This implies that a proposition or a statement is literally meaningful if it is "empirically verifiable". And Ayer holds that a proposition is "empirically verifiable" if and only if it is tested by "empirical observations". In this connection, he writes in the context of the verification principle of meaning that, *"...roughly stated, it lays it down that the meaning of a statement is determined by the way in which it can be verified, where its being verified consists in its being tested by empirical observations."*[11] So Ayer lays emphasis on the "factual significance" of propositions for it to become meaningful. He writes, *"we say that a sentence is factually significant to any given person if and only if he knows how to verify the proposition which it purports to express that is if he knows what observation would lead him under certain conditions to accept the proposition as being true, or reject it as being false.*"[12]

Ayer counts on both empirical verifiability and empirical falsifiability in order to suffice for factual and literal significance of a proposition. In other words, he derives "literal significance" from "factual significance". Consequently, he explains that a proposition is literally meaningful, if it is factually meaningful. This is because, according to him, the factual contents of a literally meaningful proposition consists only of the sense-data or sense-contents. Before we give an analysis of Ayer's factual contents which he claims to arrive at through the verification principle, let us see how he makes room within his own framework of the verification principle for

(I) the propositions regarding natural and social science

(ii) statements about the past, and

(iii) other general propositions.

While attempting to accommodate such propositions, Ayer propounds four senses of verifiability. In this connection he draws two distinctions:

Firstly, between verifiability in practice and verifiability in principle, and Secondly, between strong (conclusive) verification, and weak (probabilistic) verification and in each case he claims to choose what he regards to be the liberal alternative.

Thus in respect of the first distinction, Ayer acknowledges the significance of the proposition that there are mountains on the further side of the moon. He writes, *"No rocket has yet been invented which would enable me to go and look at the farther side of the moon, so that I am unable to decide the matter by actual observation. But I do know what observations would decide it for me, if, as is theoretically conceivable, I were once in a position to make them. And therefore I say that the proposition is verifiable in principle, if not in practice, and is accordingly significant."*[13]

We would like to pointout that since now people have landed on moon, so the proposition that "there are mountains on the other side of moon" has become verifiable even in practice. Consequently, we may replace Ayer's example of moon by that of `Saturn'.

Regarding the distinction between "strong" and "weak" sense of verifiability, Ayer holds that, *"A proposition is said to be verifiable, in the strong sense of the term, if, and only if, its truth could be conclusively established in experience. But it is verifiable, in the weak sense, if it is possible for experience to render it probable."*[14] In this context he further argues that, *"...if we adopt conclusive verifiability as our criterion of significance, we are logically obliged to treat... general propositions... in the same fashion as we treat the statements of the metaphysician."*[15] For him, in this sense of verification, many significant empirical statements cannot, even in principle, be conclusively validated or confuted. As a result he claims to use "verification" in the "weak sense". According to this sense of verifiability, he explains that factual significance will depend, not on conclusive verifiability, but merely on the possibility of favourable or unfavourable evidence. He states, "*Accordingly, we fall back on the weaker sense of verification. We say that the question that must be asked about any... statement of fact is not, would any observations make its truth or falsehood logically certain? but simply, would any observations be relevant to the determination of its truth or falsehood? And it is only if a negative answer is given to this second question that we conclude that the statement under consideration is nonsensical.*"[16]

Thus, on the basis of the "weak sense" of verifiability, Ayer attempts to provide significance to all general propositions. This is because he holds that in the "weak sense" of verification we can at least find evidence for or against such propositions.

What are these evidences which Ayer refers to? In other words, what can one verify through the principle of verification?

I have tried to show show that within Ayer's framework, one can verify only the 'objects of sensations', like the "impressions" of Hume. These 'objects of sensations', according to him are the "sense-data" or the "sense-contents". These have been interpreted as 'abstract objects of sensations' by Suman Gupta since Ayer denies the material and mental reality.

It may now be asked what is the ontological status of the sense-data or sense-contents? Are they subjective or they are objective? As we have mentioned while discussing Hume, most of the philosophers have interpreted his impressions to be objective and have consequently interpreted him to be a realist. But at the same time we have also shown that there are other philosophers who have interpreted Hume's "impressions" to be dependent on mind and considers him to be a subjective-idealist philosopher.

Coming to the question of the status of the sense-data or sense-contents, we have tried to argue in this book that the above interpretation of Hume's "impressions" can be applied to Ayer's "sense-contents" also. In other words, we have tried to show that like Hume, Ayer can also be interpreted as a subjective idealist philosopher. His own position, where the status of the objects of sensation (*i.e.*, sense-data) is concerned, is ofcourse different since he claims that these sense-data are "neutral"and thus professes to uphold a neutral monist position. According to this view sense-data are neither mental nor material entities but both matter and mind are "logical constructs" out of them. (We have discussed this issue after analysing his sense-data).

However the nuetral monist position of Ayer has been criticised by a few philosophers. Michael williams for example regards it as a metaphysical doctrine. To this effect he writes in Fact, science and morality that, "...Neutral monism is surely a *metaphysical doctrine, if any is, even by Ayer's own standards. It is hardly analytic.... It is curious to note that Ayer gives as an example of a senseless metaphysical statement the claim that the universe consists of experience, while himself holding that minds and material objects are alike logical construction out of 'neutral' sense-contents, as if semantic assent could turn metaphysical nonsense into philosophical truth.*"[17]

Let us now expound and examine Ayer's concept of sense-content or sense-data.

AYER'S SENSE-CONTENT OR SENSE-DATA

We may mention at the outset that "sense-contents" and "sense-data" have the same connotation in Ayer's philosophy. He uses the concept "sense-contents" in *Language, Truth and Logic* which he wrote in 1936. However, in the *Foundations of Empirical Knowledge* which he wrote in 1940, he uses the concept "sense-data" instead of "sense contents". He explains that we can know only the sense-data because, according to him, these are the only objects which are verified in our perception.

Thus, it appears that only sense-data, and not the material objects are verifiable, according to Ayer and so constitute the criterion of meaning in his philosophy. In this way we find that Hume's theory of truth is converted through the verification principle of meaning into a theory of meaning. In order to further support his thesis of sense-data, Ayer introduces the "argument from illusion". Hence let us now discuss this argument in order to see how on the basis of this argument he claims that sense data are the only realities, the only verifiable entities.

ARGUMENT FROM ILLUSION

On the basis of this argument, Ayer expresses the view that appearances of material things vary from one observer to another, and even to the same observer under different conditions. *"This argument, as it is ordinarily stated, is based on the fact that material things may present different appearances to different observers, or to the same observer in different conditions, and that the character of these appearances is to some extent causally determined by the state of the conditions and the observer.*"[18] This implies that sometimes we do not perceive things as they really are. In his attempt to exemplify this argument, Ayer takes an instance of a coin, which looks circular from one point of view and may look elliptical from another, or a stick which normally appears straight but looks bent when seen in water. Besides, he also takes the cases of mirror images, double vision, and complete hallucinations such as mirage, in order to provide further examples of the argument from illusion. He maintains that these illusions are not a peculiarity of visual appearances, but also occur in the "domains of other senses". According to him in cases of such appearances, one of the appearances is veridical and the other is delusive. But even in the case of delusive or non-veridical appearances, he asserts that that we still see something. This "something" is what he calls the "sense-datum". "*Nevertheless, even in the case where what we see is not the real quality of a material thing, it is supposed that we are still seeing something; and that it is convenient to give this a name. And it is for this purpose that philosophers have recourse to the term "sense-datum.*"[19] On the basis of the acceptance of sense-data or sense-contents as the immediate objects of sensation, Ayer abolishes the distinction between illusion and reality. According to him, 'reality' is nothing but appearances under 'normal' conditions. He thus tries to show that even the delusive appearances have a definite content.

He proposes other arguments to further support his denial of the distinction between appearance and reality, and his acceptance of everything that is given in sense-experience as "sense-data". In one of these arguments, he envisages that there is "*no intrinsic difference in kind between those of our perceptions that are veridical in their presentation of material things, and those that are delusive.*"[20] Thus, he argues that there is no difference between illusory and veridical perception and holds that in both the cases what is given is the same, *i.e.,* sense-data. He explains his position through the example of the amputated legs of a person and writes, "*when people whose legs have been amputated continue to feel pressure upon them, their experience is qualitatively the same as if pressure really were being exerted upon their legs.*"[21] This is so, because, he argues, that, had there been any distinction between our veridical and illusory perceptions, we would have been able to know it through our sense-experience. But since through our sense-experiences, we can know only the sense-data, therefore, he asserts that we can never know such a distinction. He writes, "*We should expect to be able to tell from the intrinsic character of a perception whether it was a perception of a sense-datum or of a material thing. But this is not possible...*"[22]

In this way we find that, on the basis of the "*argument from illusion*", *Ayer arrives at his* "*observational ontology of sense-data.*"[23] Within his semantic framework, he maintains that these sense-data are not factual entities, but they are "linguistic concepts". We may mention here that there are many other philosophers besides Ayer who have introduced sense-data in their analysis of perception. Some of the prominent among them are Betrand Russell, G.E.Moore, and H.H.Price. Hence Let us now briefly state the views of these above mentioned philosophers, on the concept of `sense-data'.

In his book *The Problems of Philosophy* (1912), Russell writes, *"Let us give a name 'sense-data' to the things that are immediately known in sensations, such as colours, sounds, smells, hardness, and so on. We shall give the name sensation to the experience of being immediately aware of these things."*[24]

G.E. Moore, explains sense-data, in the following manner. He says, *"I shall always talk of sense-data, when what I mean such things as this colour and size and shape or the patch which is of this colour and size and shape which I actually see. And when I want to talk of my seeing of them, I shall expressly call this seeing of "sense-data"; or, if I want a term which will apply equally to all these senses."*[25]

And, H.H.Price uses the method of doubt in his attempt to introduce 'sense-data'. Price writes in *Perception* *"when I see a tomato there is much that I can doubt, I can doubt whether it is a tomato that I am seeing and not a cleverly painted piece of wax. I can doubt whether there is any material thing there at all, perhaps what I took for a tomato was really a reflection; perhaps I am even the victim of some hallucination. One thing however I cannot doubt, that there exists a red patch of a round and somewhat bulgy shape, standing out from a background of other colour patches, and having a certain visual depth, and that this whole field of colour is directly present to my consciousness.... Data of this special sort are called sense-data."*[26] It follows from the above mentioned explanations of sense-data that these are nothing but what we directly and immediately expereince in our sensations.

In support of the above mentioned interpretations of sense-data by the various philosophers, Ayer writes, "*...there is a general agreement among the philosophers who make use of the term "sense-datum", or some equivalent term, that what we immediately experience is always a sense datum....*"[27]

From the way these philosophers introduce the concept of 'sense-data', in their analysis of perception, it appears that they are introducing a new fact of experience just as the way a scientist discovers a new empirical fact. As a result, a number of philosophers who claim that what we perceive in sense-experience are not the sense-data but material objects, criticize the above mentioned sense-datum theory. Some of these criticisms are based on the Gestalt psychology. According to this view, it is argued that what we perceive are not the discrete and isolated patches of colours, sounds and tastes etc. but objects as a whole, which are composed of these various patches. These philosophers maintain that it is only later on that we analyse them into their various components. For example, these philosophers hold that we first see the tree as a whole and then analyse it into its various components like its leaves, branches and so on.

Against such critical arguments based on the Gestalt psychology, Ayer argues, that the introduction of sense-data is not based upon the discovery of any new facts. In this context, while drawing analogy from the scientists, who introduce new terminologies in order to justify their analysis of a particular phenomenon, Ayer argues that like the scientists, philosophers are also justified in introducing new terminologies for their analysis of certain concepts. He thus, justifies the induction of the terminology of sense-data for the analysis of perception. This justification for Ayer, is based on the reduction of the claim to knowledge. Thus although his general position on the concept of 'sense-data' remains the same, as he propounds it in the *Foundations of Empirical Knowledge*, he introduces a new terminology of the sense-data, in *The problems of knowledge*, where he uses the expression "seeming-sense-data". He gives the example of a cigarette case lying ahead of him, and says, "*...I may, in saying that I see the cigarette case, be claiming more than the experience strictly warrants.... It may be suggested, therefore, that if I wish to give a strict account of my present visual experience, I must make a more cautious statement. I must say not that I see the cigarette case... but only that it seems to me that I am seeing it.... The next step is to convert the sentence 'it now seems to me that I see a cigarette case' into 'I am now seeing a seeming--cigarette case'. And this seeming cigarette case, which lives only in my present experience, is an example of a sense-datum.... These seeming-objects are sense-data; and the conclusion may be more simply expressed by saying that it is always sense-data that are directly perceived.*"[28]

Thus Ayer explains that sense-data can be introduced as a new terminology in the analysis of perception by reducing the claims to knowledge. These sense-data are 'private' and 'transitory', because being objects of direct awareness, their existence is logically dependent on one's own perception. This is true of Berkeley's "ideas" as well as Hume's 'impressions' as we have already stated in the chapters. Thus proceeding, the sense-data constitute the "hard-data" in Ayer's ontology, of which, as he claims, one is certain; he asserts that these sense-data or hard-data can be known without going farther than what the experience "strictly warrants". In other words, for him sense-data are free of all the interpretations, inferences, and inter-relations and are thus independent of our activities.

Charles Tayler however, charges Ayer by maintaining that, under the cover of reduction of claim to knowledge, fictitious entities *i.e.*, sense-data, replace the identifiable objective objects. He, on the other hand, argues that even after reducing the claim to knowledge, all we see are the material objects. He explains his position through the example of a murder and writes, *"We are already familiar with this in ordinary life, where on being challenged, we scale down a perceptual claim in order to have something we can really vouch for. 'Did you really see the accused stab the victim? 'Well, no, not really, but I saw him take out his knife, and gesture threateningly, and just then my attention was distracted, but I heard a cry, and there was the victim, lying on the grounds."*[29]

Taylor holds that even in these cases, "the stripped-down" claim is still a 'material-object' claim; it deals with certain objects seen, not just with the "experience of seeing." According to him, we cannot report through language our bare experience for the simple fact, that there are no corresponding objects to these experiences. He argues that what is given in experience involves the activity of man in terms of the goal involved and the selection by the subject of the objects to be perceived. That is, there can be no `hard data', in perception. This is so, because, all cognitive activities does involve some interpretation. In his words, "*...the sense-datum is an incoherent or impossible notion because there is no experience which is independent of our activity.*"[30]

Using the term "patterned activity" for all our purposeful activities, Taylor writes, "*Our phenomenal field, or the world as it appears to us, which is what our sense-datum language is supposed to describe, is what I should call patterned activity. I am introducing `patterned activity' as a term of art for purposeful activity.... Now our phenomenal field can be called a patterned activity because we cannot have a phenomenal field which is not in some way shaped by some features being objects of salient focus....*"[31] He further writes that, "*...in so far as we can characterise our perceptual experience, or the way things appear to us, it is not as a set of independent objects, but rather as a patterned activity, because this experience is not a detachable product of our activity of organisation; rather, our phenomenal field's being organised in a certain way is just our selecting, focussing, relating, identifying the things before us in the way we do.*"[32] He concludes, "*Thus, our selection-identification-organisation of perception is directed not only by our interests and desires but also by our sense of what is real, by the demands of veridicalness. And this is what makes the sense-datum language impossible. For perception yields no basic, hard, rock-bottom data which are prior to all inference or interpretation.*"[33] We thus find that Taylor denies the possibility of sense-data or any hard-data in perception.

On the other hand from Ayer's 'observational ontology

of sense-data' it is entailed that these sense data are the only objects which we are immediately aware of. In other words, this implies that through sense-experience one can verify only the sense-data. As a result a question arises that if only the sense-data are directly verifiable then what is the status of material objects in Ayer's ontology?

The question of the status of material objects is directly linked with the theory of perception. Broadly speaking there are three such theories of perception. These are:

(i) the Naive realist theory of perception, which states that we can directly perceive only the material things.

(ii) the causal theory of perception which states that we can directly perceive 'ideas' and that the material objects are the causes of these ideas. This theory is advocated by locke, as has been shown in the first chapter.

(iii) the phenomenalist theory of perception, which states that we can directly perceive the sense-data and that the material objects are logical constructions out of these sense data.

In the context of material objects, Ayer accepts the third theory. But here a problem arises for him. It may be questioned that since material things continue to exist even when they are not perceived, how can one 'construct' a material object or material thing from these sense-data, which exist only so long as they are perceived by us?

In order to interpret the construction of material things, Ayer introduces "possible sense-data", in his ontology. His reasons for introducing "possible sense data" is similar to that of Hume. As we have already stated in the second chapter, Hume introduces "ideas", besides the `impressions', in his ontology, with the same end in view i.e., to interpret the material things. Ayer explains that the possible entities become actual sense-data, only when certain conditions are fulfilled. He puts forward four such conditions which *constitute the "laws of sensory association", and "give rise to our conception of the material world".* In his own words, these conditions, may be stated as *"First, the relations of resemblance between individual sense-data; secondly, the comparative stability of the contexts in which these resemblant sense-data occur; thirdly, the fact that the occurrence of such sense-data is systematically repeatable... and fourthly, the dependence of this repetition upon the movements of the observer."*[34] So we find that whereas Hume uses "laws of association", Ayer uses "laws of sensory association" in thier respective endeavors to "construct" objects in the material world.

It thus follows that phenomenalism, as a theory of perception, attempts to interpret material things in terms of actual and possible sense-data, without there being actually a material object. In other words, it may be deciphered that the purpose of phenomenalism as a theory of perception in Ayer's philosophy is to deny the material substance. He extends his phenomenalism even in the context of the 'self', in order to deny the mental substance. It may thus be observed that underlying Ayer's introduction of the verification principle of meaning, as a "criterion of meaning", which results in his introduction of the "actual and possible sense-data" and consequent denial of both the material and the spiritual substance, is his phenomenalistic interpretation of the material objects and the self.

We shall now take up Ayer's phenomenalistic analysis of the material objects and then move on to his analysis of the "self" in similar terms.

PHENOMENALISTIC ANALYSIS OF MATERIAL OBJECTS

Phenomenalism, in Ayer's words is, *"a theory of perception" which upholds the view that "...physical objects are logical constructions out of sense-data."*[35]

So, it is obvious that through phenomenalism, Ayer, attempts to 'define' the material things in terms of sense-data or sense-contents. In this connection he writes, *"...We know that it must be possible to define material things in terms of sense-contents, because it is only by the occurrence of certain sense contents that the existence of any material thing can ever be in the least degree verified. And thus we see that we have not to inquire whether a phenomenalist "theory of perception" or some other sort of theory is correct, but only what form of phenomenalist theory is correct."*[36]

So, it ensues that for Ayer, the existence of material things is dependent on the occurrence of certain sense-contents or sense-data. But at the same time he asserts that the term *"material thing"* is not equivalent to any term or set of terms that stand for a species of sense data. *"All the same, the term "material thing" is not synonymous with any term or set of terms that stand for species of sense-data."*[37] This is because, as we have seen the ontological status of material things and that of the sense-data is not the same. However Ayer tries to cover up this problem by explaining that relation between material thing and sense-data, is "not factual but a linguistic relationship". And so he claims, *"It is... logically necessary that any situation that in any degree establishes the existence of a material thing should also establish the existence of a sense datum."*[38] While trying to explain his position he gives the example of `match box' and writes, *"If, for example, it is a fact that I am seeing a match-box,... then it follows that,... I am seeing some sense-datum." "Thus, when I say, truly as it happens, that I am now perceiving a match-box, part of what I am saying is that I am sensing sense-data of a certain kind, but only part. I am saying that and something more. But what more?.... And the phenomenalists answer to it is that the more that I am saying is that further sense-data of the appropriate sort would, in the appropriate conditions, be obtainable."*[39] This is, because, sense-data are the only observable entities in Ayer's ontology. And since it is impossible to make a transition from the observed to what he conceives, in principle, to be the unobserved, it is only through the occurrence of "further sense-data still", that the existence of a material thing can be verified. Ayer avows that *the statements about material things are equivalent to statements about sense-data. "If this is correct, then it seems to follow that the statement that I am perceiving this match-box, or whatever other physical object may be taken as an example, must be equivalent to some set of statements about sense-data."*[40]

This is "logical construction" for Ayer. He argues that it does not mean that physical objects are literally composed of sense-data. *"It means simply that statements about physical objects are somehow reducible to statements about sense-data, or as it is sometimes put, that to say anything about a physical object is to say something though not necessarily the same thing, about sense-data.*"[41]

In *Language, Truth and Logic*, he expresses a logical construction as "*...linguistic assertion, to the effect that the symbol `table' is definable in terms of certain symbols which stand for sense-contents, not explicitly, but in use. And this... is tantamount to saying that sentences which contain the symbol `table'... can all be translated into sentences of the same language which do not contain that symbol nor any of its synonyms, but do contain certain symbols which stand for sense-contents; a fact which may be loosely expressed by saying that to say anything about a table is always to say something about sense-contents.*"[42]

Thus, Ayer uses a formal mode of speech, as opposed to Hume's material mode of speech and explains that propositions about material objects can be translated into propositions about sense-data without any residue. However, he maintains that this claim can be evidently upheld, if we confine ourselves only to actual sense-data. This is because, the existence of sense-data is conditioned by our perceptions whereas, we know that material objects exist continuously. So, Ayer introduces the "possible" sense-data and the "hypothetical" propositions, within his ontological framework. In this context, he once again reverts to the example of a match box in *Philosophical Essays*, and writes, "*...this match box is not continuously perceived either by me or by anybody else. And yet at times when no one is perceiving it, that is, when there are no sense-data that are directly relevant to its existence, the match box may still exist.*"[43] He argues, it is "not self-contradictory" to say, both, that a given physical object exists in a certain place... and that no one was sensing any such sense-data which would constitute direct evidence for the existence of that object in question. He says, *"if the sense-datum language is to do the work that phenomenalists require of it, it must permit us to refer to possible sense-data. And what this means is that some at least of the statements about sense-data that are supposed to yield the equivalence of statements about physical objects will have to be hypothetical."*[44]

The hypothetical statements, according to him state *"not that any sense-data have occurred, are occurring or will occur, but that in certain specifiable conditions certain sense-data would occur."*[45] Thus, it is through the hypothetical conditions that Ayer attempts to explain the existence of the material things.

We find that, for Ayer, whereas it is both a necessary as well as sufficient condition for the existence of a sense-data that it should be actually sensed; it is neither necessary nor an altogether sufficient condition of the existence of a material thing, that it should actually be perceived. As a result, he finds statements about physical objects to be "necessarily indefinite" "at the level of sense-data". For this reason he explains that no statement about material things can be conclusively verified, *"...however much favourable evidence there may be for it, it is still always conceivable that further evidence will show it to have been false all along."*[46] He thus infers that statements about material things cannot be equivalent to any finite set of statements about sense-data. *"The reason is that all statements about physical objects are indefinite.... Consequently, the comparatively definite statements that one makes about sense-data, ... cannot be exact translations of the indefinite statements that one makes about physical objects.*"[47] We thus find that Ayer consequently changes his position in *The Problems of Knowledge*.

He writes, "*...the phenomenalists programme cannot be carried through. Statements about physical objects are not formally translatable into statements about sense-data.*"[48]

Let us now take up Ayer's phenomenalistic analysis of the 'Self'.

AYER'S PHENOMENALISTIC ANALYSIS OF THE SELF

Coming to the question of the phenomenalistic analysis of the 'Self', Ayer like Hume claims to reduce 'self' to sense-contents or sense-data. He writes, "*We know that a self, if it is not to be treated as a metaphysical entity, must be held to be a logical construction out of sense-experience. It is, in fact a logical construction which constitutes the actual and possible sense-history of the self.*"[49]

He asserts that these sense-experiences out of which the notion of 'self' is derived must belong to the sense-history of the same 'self'. "*...it is logically impossible for a sense-experience to belong to the sense-history of more than a single self.*"[50]

We thus find, as we have mentioned in the case of Hume, the 'self', in Ayer's ontology is a "bundle" of these private experiences. "*...I can have direct knowledge of my own experiences and that I cannot have direct knowledge* *of anyone else's... the point is that if the statement which expresses what I claim to know refers only to my present experience, I am in the best possible position to decide its truth. If I judge it to be true, it is on the basis of an experience which conclusively verifies it....*"[51]

He further argues that even if it is granted that others besides 'myself' come to know about my experiences, their knowledge will not be 'direct'. *"For it can be founded only upon experiences of their own, and however strongly these experiences favour the truth of the statement about my experience, they do not establish it conclusively."* Thus Ayer concludes, *"The reason why I cannot directly know the experiences of another person is simply that I cannot have them."*[52]

On the basis of the above arguments, it seems to follow that for Ayer, only one's private experiences are directly verifiable and so one can know only such experiences.

He explains that we generally claim that we have perceived the same object, but it is not so. This is because, the object we perceive are physical objects and there are as many perceptions of them as there are number of people observing them. *"There is a good and familiar sense in which two different people may be said to perceive the same object, hear the same sound, feel the same feeling, and from this it follows that they do have the same experiences. But, it will be answered, even though they may perceive the same objects,... they do not sense the same sense-data: the sense-data which they respectively sense may be qualitatively similar but they cannot be numerically the same."*[53] This is because he argues, *"...the sense-data are made private by definition; they are characterized in such a way that the statement that one person has another's sense-data describes no possible situation.*"[54]

It is thus made clear by Ayer, that the various experiences that each person undergoes while perceiving an object are private to his own self. In this context he writes in *The Problems of Knowledge*, "*It is maintained... that two different persons perceiving the same physical object is `really' a matter of each one's sensing his own sense data; and these sense-data, though they may be similar, cannot be the same. And so we reach the philosophical contention that all one's experiences are private to oneself.*"[55]

Ayer's position is thus that of solipsism. As a result the question arises that if all the experiences are 'private' to us, then (i) how do we know the existence of other people? (ii) how can we have the knowledge of the other minds?

Let us first discuss Ayer's analysis of the existence of other people.

Ayer attempts to interpret the existence of other people following a reductive analysis, in *Language, Truth and Logic*, just as he attempts to interpret the existence of material things and the 'self' in his ontology. He writes, "*And just as I must define material things and my own self in terms of their empirical manifestations, so I must define other people in terms of their empirical manifestations, that is, in terms of the behaviour of their bodies, and ultimately in terms of sense-contents.*"[56]

Thus in conformity with his verification principle of meaning and the resultant ontology of sense-data or sense-contents, he tries to give a meaning to the existence of other people in terms of their 'bodily behaviour', which he further interprets in term of "sense-contents". He says, *"And thus I find that I have as good a reason to believe in the existence of other people as I have to believe in the existence of material things. For in each case my hypothesis is verified by the occurrence in my sense-history of the appropriate series of sense-contents."*[57]

The above account clearly shows that one can only have knowledge of ones sense-contents *"...each of us has to define the contents of another man's sense experience in terms of what he can himself observe."*[58]

But how do these sense-contents or the various experiences explain the 'identity' of a person?

Ayer attempts to provide an answer to this problem in *The Problems of Knowledge* by evolving what he considers a "general criterion of personal identity". He says, *"Indeed it would seem that there have to be such criteria if our talk of persons is to have any meaning at all?"*[59] He calls it a "practical approach" for recognising people. He asks how do we succeed in recognising people? What makes me say that a man whom I can now see is the same man whom I had seen a week ago? He says that the probable answer is that he "looks the same". This implies, according to Ayer, that there is "a fairly close resemblance between the appearance of this man and the appearance of the man I saw last week". This resemblance is what constitutes the "practical method of identification", according to Ayer. He uses this method, to convey not only the "personal identity" of his own self and the "bodily identity" of the person seen. He seems to accept the first, because the opposite will lead to an absurdity, and the second, because he explains that a person can be known only through the perception of his body.

We may mention here that Ayer does not consider this to be a logical method of identification. He only claims it to be practical and clear way of establishing the personal identity. He writes, *"The fact that people's physical characteristics tend to be distinctive and that many constant features commonly persist through out what is only a gradual process of changes, makes this,... a practical method of identification. As a criterion it is however neither necessary nor sufficient."*[60] In this way he tries to establish, the identity of a person through the identity of his body. *"In this sense... the identity of a person is founded on the identity of his body."*[61]

We thus notice a shift in Ayer's own position regarding phenomenalism. Whereas he offers phenomenalistic interpretation in the context of self, he does not continue with it, in the context of "personal identity" of a person. He writes, in *The Problems of Knowledge*, *"And if the sense-data have to be defined in terms of persons, and the identity of persons is itself derived from the identity of their bodies, then the analysis of physical identity in terms of relations between sense-data would appear to create a vicious circle. Failing a wholly different account of personal identity, the only way of escape would be to deny that sense-datum have to be defined in terms of persons...."*[62]

In this way by defining 'personal identity' in terms

of 'bodily identity', Ayer claims to "solve" Hume's problem of personal identity of the self. We have already discussed that Hume could not explain the notion of single self, through personal identity, and so he introduced 'memory' in order to explain the single 'self'.

Ayer on the other hand claims that memory is not sufficient. *He writes, "It needs to be backed by some other relation... the relation that holds between experiences when they are constituents of the same consciousness."* This relation according to Ayer is derived from the existence of one's body. *"The alternative is to regard.... that a person's existence is tied to the existence of his body."*[63]

Thus Ayer claims to solve Hume's problem of the 'personal identity', through the introduction of 'bodily identity'.

In this context he writes, *"...we have solved Hume's problem by defining personal identity in terms of bodily identity, and bodily identity is to be defined in terms of the resemblance and continuity of sense-contents."*[64]

Suman Gupta, however, interprets the position of Hume and Ayer on the above mentioned issue to be the same. In this context she says, *"Ayer... introduced 'body' only to collect 'sense-contents' as belonging to one self," on the basis of 'resemblance' and 'continuity' of sense-contents".... Actually there is no difference between the position of Hume and Ayer."*[65]

Let us now take up Ayer's analysis of one's knowledge of the other minds, since it is closely associated with his analysis of the existence of other people.

KNOWLEDGE OF OTHER MINDS

Ayer's analysis of the knowledge of other minds logically follows from his rejection of the phenomenalistic analysis of the existence of other people, which we have discussed above. He argues that one can distinguish his own thoughts, feelings and their outward manifestations but in no way, one can only distinguish others thoughts, feelings and their outward manifestations. This is so, because, he explains, one can only observe the outward manifestation of other people's behaviour. He writes, "*There can be no empirical grounds for inferring the occurrence of behaviours, on the part of other people, which one is not actually observing, in as much as it is logically conceivable that one should observe it, but there cannot, on this view, be any empirical grounds for inferring the existence of anything "behind" this behaviour of which it might be supposed to be an external manifestation.*"[66]

Thus, he conveys that the physical manifestation of other people's behaviour doesnot provide any grounds for inferring the existence of anything that is not given in one's own sense-contents. This is once again because of his verification principle which constitutes the core of his epistemology, and promotes the ontology of appearances alone.

In *Philosophical Essays*, he tries to solve the problem of the knowledge of other minds through telepathy and argument from analogy. Hence let us briefly discuss these methods.

TELEPATHY

Telepathy is regarded as a type of extra sensory

perception through which one can introspect into others minds. Ayer holds that by telepathy one can read the thoughts of others directly, without employing any physical means *"What is strange about telepathy is that a message is transmitted, apparently without the employment of any physical means."*[67] Nevertheless, he expresses that even these experiences are personal and argues that although a person who practices telepathy can know what is going on in other's mind he still cannot share his thoughts or feelings.

"...to be informed of another's feelings telepathically is not to share it; and even if it were to share it, there would be exactly the same grounds here as in the case of any other's shared feelings for saying that there were two feelings and not one."[68] The question of sharing other's mental phenomena does not arise, in Ayer's ontological framework, because of each individual's restricted private experiences.

ARGUMENT FROM ANALOGY

The argument from analogy as expounded by Ayer proceeds from the assumption that it is supposed that the way we note the connections between our own states of mind and their outward expressions, likewise we also notice these outward expressions in others. As a result, he holds that there must be some connection between their outward expressions and states of mind. He argues, *"By analogy with what I have observed of other people and what I have learnt about myself, I infer that some one with the relevant sort of nervous system, when operated on in such and such conditions, will show signs of pain, signs that I may well be able to detect if I watch him closely enough. But then*

I want to go further and argue from the existence of these signs to the existence of his actual feeling of pain, which exhypothesi, since it is not my feeling, I cannot detect."[69]

He further explains this argument through the example of pain resulting from extracting a tooth. He explains, when I am having an infected tooth, I go to a dentist and get it removed. In such a condition I maintain that my feeling of pain when dentist operates on me will provide me with a reason for believing that my friend feels pain when the dentist operates on him. However, he argues that the pain experienced by me and that experienced by my friend cannot be the same. He claims that it is only because I experienced the pain, that I believe that my friend too is in pain.

He holds that an argument from analogy is valid, only when there is a possibility of establishing the existence of other minds. Thus he expresses the futility of the argument in the following manner, "*An important consequence of this argument, if it is sound, is that we must give up the argument from analogy on which many people have relied as a justification for believing in the existence of other minds. It is tempting to think that one can come of the idea of one's own experiences of certain kinds are characteristically associated with certain forms of behaviour.... Assuming it is logically impossible for anyone directly to observe what goes on in another persons mind, some philosophers have maintained that this is not a valid argument from analogy, for they hold that no inductive argument can give us any reason to believe in the existence of something which could not even in principle be observed.*"[70]

Thus we find that even the argument from analogy fails to justify the knowledge of other minds in Ayer's ontological framework. This is because, his verification principle takes into account only such knowledge as are given in sense-experience. In other words for Ayer there can be no experience, even in principle, of any knowledge of the other minds. We can only know what is happening in others mind by linking their mental happenings to some of their perceptible behaviour.

Ayer's denial of both the material things as well as the 'self' and consequently his phenomenalist reduction of the material things and the 'self' into the actual and possible sense-data or sense-contents seems to give rise to two important logical consequences within his philosophical framework.

Firstly, this implies a denial of the category of substance and consequently a denial of the dynamic and causally interconnected objective material reality. As a result we find that there is no scope of a certain and universal knowledge within his ontological framework. Therefore, he claims that synthetic propositions are all probable, and in support of his view he writes, "all propositions which have a factual content can best be a probable hypotheses."

The second consequence, which logically follows from his empirical manifestation of the material things and the self in terms of observable sense data, is a subsequent denial of supersensible reality. Thus he claims to reject metaphysics.

It appears to us that Ayer not only denies metaphysics as a super-sensible reality, but as Suman Gupta maintains, he also rejects it as a "world view".

Suman Gupta interprets three senses of the concept of 'metaphysics', all of which are linked together. These three senses are as follows:

(i) metaphysics as a world-view

(ii) metaphysics as a study of supersensible reality, and

(iii) metaphysics understood as an abstract system."[71]

According to Suman Gupta, the concept of metaphysics as a world-view is derived from Aristotle's definition of metaphysics. She holds "Metaphysics, for Aristotle, is the "First philosophy" which deals with the theoretical aspects of reality *i.e.,* the Being, its components, causes and origin. According to her, taken in this sense, there is much in common between metaphysics on the one hand and science on the other. For, she maintains, "both science and philosophy are not concerned with particular things or processes but with the "general laws of development of nature and society." She further writes, "According to this view the basic difference between science and metaphysics consists in the fact that whereas science is confined only to one aspect of reality, metaphysics,... provides a holistic view of the world." Thus, Suman Gupta concludes that metaphysics as a 'world-view' not only accepts the existence of objective reality but also includes `man's capacity to transform the world.'

Since Ayer denies the objective material reality it follows, according to the above interpretation, that he subsequently denies "metaphysics" as a world-view.

According to the second sense, metaphysics is

interpreted as a study of the supersensible reality, that transcends the limits of sensory observations. According to this sense, as maintained by Suman Gupta, "Metaphysics... is completely divorced from the world of sense experience and practical life."

We find that Ayer uses the verification principle of meaning in order to reject this sense of metaphysics as being "meaningless" or "non-sensical". He writes, in this connection, *"no statement which refers to a `reality' transcending the limits of all possible sense-experience can possibly have any literal significance."*[72] He further explains in this context that, *"...metaphysical sentence... express neither a tautology nor an empirical hypothesis. And as tautologies and empirical hypotheses form the entire class of significant propositions, we are justified in concluding that all metaphysical assertions are nonsensical."*[73]

Besides, the above mentioned senses, Suman Gupta states forward a third sense, in which metaphysics is understood as an "abstract system". "Metaphysics" understood in this sense means, "a system where an aspect of reality is abstracted from its totality and is assigned an independent existence." She maintains that the second and third connotations of the concept metaphysics are interrelated *"...those who assert the existence of supersensible reality are metaphysicians in the third sense as well because they abstract consciousness in the form of God or soul etc., from its objective material totality and posit it in the supersensible world. But in the third sense the mechanical materialists are equally metaphysicians because they divorce matter from consciousness and attempt to explain man only as a biological being."*[74]

After giving the above stated exposition of metaphysics, let us now assess Ayer's entire philosophy, as presented in this chapter. We shall assess his philosophy both within the stream of analytic philosophy, and outside the stream of analytic philosophy. Here we shall mainly examine the verification principle of meaning, and his phenomenalism.

Since the verification principle is based on the division of analytic and synthetic propositions let us first examine this division.

CRITICISMS OF THE ANALYTIC-SYNTHETIC DIVISION AND AYER'S VERIFICATION PRINCIPLE

The most notable objection against the analytic-synthetic division and verification principle within the analytical circle was raised by W.V. Quine in his paper "Two dogmas of empiricism" (1953). Here the two dogmas referred to that of "analyticity" and "reductionism" and were both rejected by Quine. Regarding "analyticity" he attacks the criterion of definition which is pivotal to it and captures synonym *i.e.,* sameness of linquistic meaning. He, however finds the notion of synonymy to be an obscure one and charges the attempts to define "analyticity" in terms of synonymy to be circular since both belong to the same family. On the other hand, he maintains that definition cannot be taken as a ground for synonymy. He writes *"Certainly the `definition' which is the lexicographer's report of an observed synonymy cannot be taken as the ground for synonymy."*[75]

While rejecting the second dogma *i.e.,* reductionism, he in agreement with Pierre Duhem contends that statements about the external world face the tribunal of sense-experience not in isolation but in groups. Such statements do not occur alone but constitute part of a more general theory. Consequently if there is a change at the observation-level, it gets reflected in the theory also. Thus Quine declares that no propositions are immune to revision-not even the analytic ones. In other words, he claims that there are no analytic truths. It is for the above stated position that Quine is often regarded as a radical empiricist.

Michaell Williams considers this distinction to be "metaphysically loaded". In Fact, Science and Morality, he writes, "*...Ayer's version of the distinction connected as it is with the analytic/synthetic distinction and the linguistic theory of necessary truth is clearly metaphysically loaded. The supposed elimination of metaphysics in favour of analysis seems as though it may well depend on substantial metaphysical commitments.*"[76]

Outside the realm of analytic philosophy, Suman Gupta disagrees with this distinction. She writes, "*...the watertight distinction between analytic and synthetic propositions is not a valid one.*" According to her "*knowledge is a synthesis of the linguistic-conceptual apparatus and experience. And experience includes both the theoretical and the practical aspects of knowledge. Thus language and logic cannot be divorced from reality.*"[77] As opposed to Ayer and other logical positivists, she holds that validity of mathematics and logic "*lies in the applicability to the objective world*" and to "*grasp the dynamic objective reality respectively.*"[78]

Let us now assess Ayer's verification principle. As we have seen he uses the weak sense of verifiability in his epistemology. It has been objected by philosophers that this sense of the term tends to make all the propositions as meaningful irrespective of their status.

Ayer claims to solve this problem by introducing the term 'observation-statement' in place of 'experiential proposition' and by providing a recursive definition of verifiability. According to this definition he holds, *"a statement is directly verifiable if it is either itself an observation statement; or is such that in conjunction with one or more observation-statements it entails at least one observation-statement which is not deducible from these premises alone, and... a statement is indirectly verifiable if it satisfies the following conditions: first, that in conjunction with certain other premises it entails one or more directly verifiable statements which are not deducible from these other premises alone: and secondly, that these other premises do not include any statement that is not either analytic, or directly verifiable, or capable of being independently established as indirectly verifiable. And I can now reformulate the principle of verification as requiring of a literally meaningful statement, which is not analytic, that it should be either directly or indirectly verifiable in the foregoing sense."*[79]

Ayer's verification principle of meaning has been interpreted as "metaphysical", by Michael Williams. Williams writes in this context, *"The most serious objection is that, in itself, the Principle is utterly vacuous. To say that a sentence is significant only if it is verifiable is to say nothing whatever until we spell out what we understand by verification. The Principle thus derives all its critical force from the radical empiricism Ayer reads into it, and it is his radical empiricism that pushes him into metaphysics.*"[80]

In another criticism, John Wisdom questions the status of the verification Principle, whether it is an empirical proposition or a tautology? He contends that the verification principle has been formulated in such a way that it is full of ambiguity. It is neither empirically verifiable nor a tautology. Thus he concludes that it is one of the metaphysical utterances. He writes, *"well, shall we accept the verification principle? What is it to accept it? When people bring out with a dashing air of the words, `The meaning of a statement is... the method of its verification, like one who says `The value of a thing is... its power of exchange'; in what sort of way are they using words? What is the general nature of their theory? The answer is `it is a metaphysical theory.*"[81]

John Foster interprets the criterion of literal significance as "imposing a very stringent criterion of significance on assertoric discourse". He refers to Ayer's criterion of *"factual significance"* and writes, *"it assumes that a person's evaluation of his observational evidence is always rational. It assumes that someone has actually verified (or falsified) a proposition if his observations lead him to accept or reject it. And this assumption is clearly false.*"[82]

In this context Suman Gupta, outside the sphere of analytic philosophy brings out the 'solipsistic content' inherent in the verification principle. She writes *"the above account of 'verifiability' implies that words in our language cannot refer to anything but the content of our sensory experience".* On the other hand she claims that 'knowledge is always the knowledge of the objective reality and 'sensing our sensation', being an abstraction, is not possible." Thus she concludes *that the verification principle of meaning is based upon the "misinterpretation of such concepts as 'knowledge', 'sense-experience' and 'verification' and that logical positivists interpret these concepts from a solipsistic point of view.*"[83]

Ayer seems to have realised this fault in his analysis of the 'verifiability principle'.

In 'Replies' in *Perception and Identity*, he writes, "*...we failed to make it clear, even to ourselves, whether the method of verification had to lie within the possible resources of the person who was interpreting the proposition or to speak more accurately, the sentence which was designed to express it... could be construed in a more impersonal and therefore liberal fashion.*"[84]

The misinterpretation of the concept of verification is also pointed out by Maurice Cornforth in the following words: "*...they assumed that what verifies a proposition is not the activity, or the whole process, of verification, but simply the sense-data which result from it.*"[85]

The aforementioned are some of the grave objections, which the principle of verification, fails to meet.

Besides these theoretical faults, it appears to us that the verification principle also derecognizes most of the meaningful statements which are aimed at social and practical reforms. Thisi s because verification, according to our view, also includes practical activities which a man performs while interacting with his surroundings. Be it as teachers, students, parents or scientists, we are always verifying issues in terms of experimentations and observations. Ayer and other positivists, on the other hand tend to confine verification only to occurence of certain appcarances thus giving it a solitary connotation.

It will not be out of place to mention at this point that Karl Popper abandons the verification criterion of the positivists and offers a critirion of falsifiability. In *The Logic of Scientific Discovery* (1980), he states that a theory is scientific only if it is falsifiabl e or refutable. He claims that knowledge grows through refutation of hypotheses that are either logically inconsistent or empirically refuted..

CRITICISMS AGAINST AYER'S PHENOMENALISM

Ayer's thesis of phenomenalism has been criticised by Isaiah Berlin. Berlin holds that phenomenalism makes "actualities depend upon possibilities". As a result, he claims, that the task of analysing material object statement would be a lengthy enterprise and therefore cannot be carried out in principle. In other wards, it is logically impossible to reduce material object statements to the statements about sense-data. He writes, *"A categorical existential material object sentence as `the table is next door' or `there is a table next door' is used at the very least to describe something which is occurring or being characterised at the time of speaking... and being characterised or occurring, unless the contrary is specifically stated or implied, not intermittently but continuously and in any case not "hypothetically". For to say something is occurring hypothetically is a very artificial and misleading way of saying, that it is not in the ordinary sense, occurring at all...."*[86]

It ensues fromthe above passage that hypothetical statements result from the reductin of material object statements to those of sense data. According to him both the sets of statements entail each other but are semantically unidentical.

On the basis of Ayer's phenomenalistic analysis of material things, his position has been interpreted as a subjective-idealist-pluralist one, outside the framework of linguistic philosophy. In this context Suman Gupta writes, *"we find that the denial of `material substance' and the assertion of 'sense-contents' entails a subjective-idealist position. And further-more since the "sense-contents" for Ayer, are discrete and transitory, his position also embodies pluralism. In short, ontologically speaking, Ayer's position is subjective-idealistic-pluralism."*[87]

In this connection while bringing out the contradiction between what Ayer claims to be doing and what he actually does, she writes, *"...here we find that contrary to the claims of Ayer that philosophy is concerned only with the analysis of language, through his philosophical analysis, he propounded a subjective-idealist pluralist world-view."*[88]

Similarly Michael Williams writes, *"whatever Ayer says, phenomenalism smacks of subjective-idealism. Neutral monism is just an uneasy attempt to gloss over the awkwardness this creates."*[89] He criticizes phenomenalism as the "Central metaphysical doctrine" of *Language, Truth and Logic* and writes, *"Indeed, it is ironic that, at a distance of 50 years, Language, Truth and Logic reads like a paradigm metaphysical tract,... phenomenalism being its central metaphysical doctrine."*[90]

We may conclude our present chapter in the following manner.

The above account of Ayer's verification principle of meaning as well as his phenomenalism imply that the sense-contents and sense-data are the ultimate units of his philosophy. And since these "sense-data", being mere 'sensations', are `mental', we find that Ayer assumes the mental side of Descartes' dualism.

On the basis of the above discussion it seems to us that Ayer, advocates phenomenalism in order to deny the category of substance which includes a denial of both the 'material' objects and the 'self', and consequently to arrive at the 'observational ontology' of sense-data or sense-contents. This is precisely because his verification principle which constitutes his epistemology and ontology is restricted to appearances alone. As a result Ayer claims his approach to be scientific. Science for him thus seems to be setting a standard for cognitive significance. Therefore whatever cannot be assimilated as science, Ayer tends to reject it as metaphysics.

But is Ayer's approach really scientific? Suman Gupta interprets Ayer to be anti-scientific. Her interpretations are based on his denial of the category of substance. She writes, *"The denial of substance, both in terms of mental and material entities, logically implies the denial of the whole gamut of scientific knowledge."*[91] This is because according to her scientific knowledge makes the following assumptions:

(i) "There is one objective-reality-natural and social

- which exists independently of human consciousness.

(ii) There are necessary causal connections in the objective reality.

(iii) Man gains knowledge of the causal connections through his practical activity.

(iv) Through this knowledge Man acquires the ability to effectively intervene in the objective reality by transforming or controlling it."[92]

She holds that the denial of substance implies the denial of all the above stated four assumptions.

On the basis of 'sense contents' being the only objects of sensations, Suman Gupta holds that scientific knowledge for them (logical positivists) consists only of a series of "sense contents" or "sense-data", which "furnish us with necessary causal connections". Thus according to her Ayer and the logical positivists 'misinterpret' sciences.

She interprets Ayer's sense-contents as 'mental' entities and consequently construes his philosophy as 'pluralist-subjective idealist' like that of Hume. And, in this sense we find that Ayer is also a metaphysician, in the third-sense because he 'abstracts' the sense-contents, from their 'material and mental reality and absolutises it'.

Similarly, Michael Williams also seems to differ from Ayer's contentions that whatever can be observed is scientifically real and also his claim that only scientific discourse is cognitively significant. He says, *"Nor will the observation that in science we only talk about such and* *such kinds of things by itself sustain the conclusion that nothing else is `really real', still less the conclusion that no form of discourse other than the scientific is cognitively significant.*"[93]

"We must conclude that Language, Truth and Logic is informed throughout by what can only be called a primitive metaphysical intuition, to the effect that the sort of facts discovered by natural sciences are all the facts there are. What the book offers is more properly described as an elevation of science to the rank of metaphysics than an elimination of metaphysics in favour of science."[94]

He further concludes, "*Making science the sole arbiter of what there really is inevitably creates pressure to espouse a physicalist ontology, which cannot really be harmonized with Ayer's ontology of sense-contents.*"[95]

REFERENCES

1. Suman Gupta, "Linguistic Philosophy-Its Social Implications", *Language and Literature in Society* (New Delhi), vol.5, Monsoon 1977 and Winter 1977-78, pp.107-12.
2. A.J. Ayer, *Language, Truth and Logic* (Preface to first edition) (London 1975), 2nd ed., p.41.
3. A.J. Ayer, in Barry Gower, ed., *Logical Positivism in Perspective* (London, 1987), p.24.
4. J.S. Mill, *Systems of Logic* (London, 1965).
5. A.J. Ayer, *Language, Truth and Logic*, op.cit., p.105.
6. *Ibid.*, p. 100.
7. *Ibid.*
8. *Ibid.*, p. 105.
9. *Ibid.*, p. 100.

10. A.J. Ayer, *op.cit.*, p. 7.
11. A.J. Ayer "The Vienna Circle", in A.J. Ayer (ed), *The Revolution in Philosophy* (London, 1963), p. 74.
12. A.J. Ayer, *Language, Truth and Logic, op.cit.*, p. 48.
13. *Ibid,* p. 49.
14. *Ibid,* p. 50.
15. *Ibid*, p. 50.
16. *Ibid,* p. 52.
17. Michael Williams, "The Elimination of Metaphysics", in Graham Macdonald and Crispin Wright (eds.), *Fact, Science and Morality* (New York, 1986), p. 13.
18. A.J. Ayer, *Foundations of Empirical Knowledge* (London, 1971), p. 3.
19. *Ibid.*, p. 4.
20. *Ibid.*, pp. 5-6.
21. *Ibid.*, p. 6.
22. *Ibid.*
23. Barry Gower, "Criterion of Significance", in Barry Gower (ed.), *op.cit.*, p. 16.
24. Bertrand Russell, *The Problem of Philosophy* (London, 1912), p. 17.
25. G.E.Moore, *Some Main Problems of Philosophy* (New York, 1966), p. 45.
26. H.H.Price, *Perception* (London, 1961), p. 3.
27. A.J. Ayer, *The Foundations of Empirical Knowledge*, op.cit., p. 5.
28. A.J. Ayer, *The Problems of Knowledge* (London, 1984), p. 96.

29. Charles Taylor in "Sense-data Revisited" in G.F.Macdonald (ed.), *Perception and Identity* (London, 1979), p. 101.
30. *Ibid.*, p. 104.
31. *Ibid.*
32. *Ibid.*, p. 106.
33. *Ibid.*
34. A.J. Ayer, *Foundations of Empirical Knowledge*, *op.cit.*, p. 259.
35. A.J. Ayer, *Philosophical Essays* (London, 1965), p. 125.
36. A.J. Ayer, *Language, Truth and Logic*, *op.cit.*, p. 71.
37. A.J. Ayer, *Foundations of Empirical Knowledge*, *op.cit.*, p. 229.
38. *Ibid.*, p. 230.
39. A.J. Ayer, *Philosophical Essays*, *op.cit.*, p. 132.
40. *Ibid.*, p. 132.
41. *Ibid.*, p. 133.
42. A.J. Ayer, *Language Truth and Logic*, *op.cit.*, pp. 85-86.
43. A.J. Ayer, *Philosophical Essays*, *op.cit.*, p. 133.
44. *Ibid.*, p. 133.
45. *Ibid.*, p. 134.
46. *Ibid.*, p.135.
47. *Ibid.*, p.140.
48. A.J. Ayer, *The Problems of Knowledge*, *op.cit.*, p. 122.
49. A.J. Ayer, *Language, Truth and Logic*, *op.cit.*, p. 165.
50. *Ibid.*, p. 166.
51. A.J.Ayer, *Philosophical Essays*, op.cit., pp.193-4.
52. *Ibid.*, p.194.

53. *Ibid.*, p.194.

54. *Ibid.*

55. A.J. Ayer, *The Problems of Knowledge*, op.cit., pp. 199-200.

56. A.J. Ayer, *Language, Truth and Logic*, op.cit., p. 171.

57. *Ibid.*, p. 171.

58. *Ibid.*, p. 174.

59. A.J. Ayer, *The Problems of Knowledge, op.cit.*, p. 188.

60. *Ibid.*, pp. 188-9.

61. *Ibid.*, p. 189.

62. *Ibid.*, p. 190.

63. *Ibid.*, p. 199.

64. A.J. Ayer, *Language, Truth and Logic, op.cit.*, p. 168.

65. Suman Gupta, *Twentieth Century Philosophy, op.cit.*, pp. 17 18.

66. A.J. Ayer, *Foundations of Empirical Knowledge, op.cit.*, p. 163.

67. A.J. Ayer, *Philosophical Essays, op.cit.*, p. 196.

68. *Ibid.*

69. *Ibid.*, p. 202.

70. A.J. Ayer, "The Concept of a Persons", in A.J. Ayer, *The Concept of a Person and Other Essays* (London, 1973), p. 87.

71. These senses of "metaphysics" have been brought out by Suman Gupta in "Metaphysics and the Verification Principle of Meaning - An Appraisal", published in the *Visva-Bharati Journal of Philosophy*, vol.31, no.1, August 1994, pp. 39-42.

72. A.J. Ayer, *Language, Truth and Logic*, *op.cit.*, p. 46.
73. *Ibid.*, p. 56.
74. Suman Gupta, in "Metaphysics and Verification Principle of Meaning - An Appraisal", *op.cit.*, p. 42.
75. W.V. Quine, "Two Dogmas of Empiricism", in Thomas M.Olschewsky (ed.) *Problems in the Philosophy of Language* (London, 1969), p. 402.
76. Michael Williams, "Elimination of Metaphysics", in Graham Macdonald and Crispin Wright (eds.), *Fact, Science and Morality* (New York, 1986), p. 10.
77. Suman Gupta, "Bertrand Russell and A.J. Ayer: A Dialectico-Materialist Approach", *Marxian Sociology* (New Delhi), vol.2, p. 310.
78. *Ibid.*
79. A.J. Ayer, *Language, Truth and Logic*, *op. cit.*, p. 17.
80. Michael Williams, "Elimination of Metaphysics", *op.cit.*, p. 10.
81. John Wisdom, "Metaphysics and Verification", *Mind*, N.S., vol. 47, no. 47, 1936, p. 454.
82. John Foster, *A.J.Ayer The Arguments of the Philosophers* (ed) Ted Honderich (London, 1985), pp. 11-12.
83. Suman Gupta, "Bertrand Russell and A.J.Ayer - A Dialectico-Materialist Approach", *op.cit.*, p. 311.
84. A.J. Ayer, "Replies", in G.F.Macdonald (ed.), *Perception and Identity* (London, 1979), p. 325.
85. Maurice Cornforth, *Science and Idealism* (New York, 1947), p. 128.
86. Isaiah Berlin, "Empirical Propositions and Hypothetical Statements", *Mind*, N.S., vol. 59, no. 59, 1950, p. 235.

87. Suman Gupta, "A.J. Ayer - A Loss to the World of Philosophy", *op. cit.*, p. 302.
88. *Ibid.*
89. Michael Williams, *Fact, Science and Morality*, *op.cit.*, p. 21.
90. *Ibid.*, p. 12.
91. Suman Gupta, "Metaphysics and the Verification Principle of Meaning - An Appraisals", *op.cit.*, p. 47.
92. *Ibid.*
93. *Ibid.*, p. 21.
94. *Ibid.*
95. *Ibid.*

5

A CRITICAL ANALYSIS OF HUME AND AYER'S CONCEPT OF CAUSATION

Although we have discussed the epistemology and ontology of David Hume and A.J. Ayer in the earlier chapters, even then, causation - which is a core concept of epistemology - requires a separate analysis. This is because, there are philosophers and among them are Hume and Ayer, who deny the necessary causal connection and consequently deny the possibility of knowledge. On the other hand, there are other philosophers who accept a necessary causal connection and consequently accept the possibility of knowledge. Therefore, we in this chapter, propose to give a critical analysis of the concept of causation, as expounded by Hume and Ayer. In the process we shall try to argue that Hume's and Ayer's views of causation can be seen in a different light from the scientific view of causation. Before we go into the details of this discussion, let us first ask the question, what is causation.

WHAT IS CAUSATION?

The concept of causation is fundamental to any

scientific knowledge. Scientific knowledge emerges and develops precisely because, there is a constant interaction of phenomena, in the objective material reality. Because of this interaction, some phenomena give rise to the others. This constitutes causation in the objective reality. The group of interacting phenomenon is called the cause: and the phenomenon produced by the action of the cause constitutes the effect. Although this implies that the cause precedes the effect, the relation of cause and effect is not a time-bound relation. In other words, succession in time is not an adequate sign of cause. For example day follows night, but night is not the cause of the day. The alteration of day and night is caused by the rotation of earth around its axis.

Moreover, the concept of causation involves the concept of 'substance', wherein the relation of cause and effect takes place. It also includes change from 'quantity to quality' as well as the categories of 'appearance' and 'essence', in cause being the essence of all the appearances. Besides, the concept of 'power' or force is also imbibed in the relation of cause and effect, in "cause" being the active power (This position, as we have seen is held by Locke).

The above mentioned essential and scientific aspects of causation are denied by both Hume and Ayer. For them causation is nothing but a relation of before and after. This follows logically from their ontological position, which is a pluralist one. They thus separate the cause from the effect. Hence let us now examine the views of causation as expounded by both these philosophers. We shall first examine Hume's view of causation.

HUME'S VIEW OF CAUSATION

Hume, in his ontology attempts to explain away the necessary causal connection through the relations of "contiguity" and "succession" among the various "events". We may point out here, as we have mentioned in the second chapter that "events" and "impressions", have the same connotation in Hume's epistemology and ontology. He uses the expression "events" in the context of causation, and while reducing material objects to `objects of sensations', he uses the expression "impressions". Thus Hume tries to establish causal link between the various events through contiguity and succession among the events. Regarding the relation of "contiguity" he writes, *"I find in the first place, that whatever objects are considered as causes and effects, are contiguous; and that nothing can operate in a time or place, which is ever so little removed from those of its existence. Though distant objects may sometimes seem productive of each other, they are commonly found upon examination to be linked by a chain of causes, which are contiguous among themselves, and to the distant objects.... We may therefore consider the relation of contiguity as essential to that of causation.*"[1]

He interprets succession as priority of time in the cause and writes, *"The second relation I shall observe as essential to causes and effects, is... that of priority of time in the cause before the effect.*"[2] This temporal succession among the events is important, according to Hume, because he maintains that in the absence of the relation of succession, all objects or "events" would become co-existent. It seems to us that Hume cannot talk of "co-existence" of "events" or "impressions" since he denies the category of substance.

For him, the category of substance, as we have already mentioned in the second chapter is only a "bundle" or "collection" of various fleeting "impressions". Since these impressions are fleeting, an impression or event cannot be contemporary to another impression or event. It can only be said that an event is *"temporaly prior" or later to another event or impression.* Therefore, Hume in his ontology, attempts to explain a causal relation through the concept of temporal priority. *In this context he writes, "...if one cause were contemporary with its effect, and this effect with its effect and so on, it is plain there would be no such thing as succession, and all objects must be co-existent."*[3]

Thus Hume uses the relations of "contiguity" and "temporal succession" to show how one event follows the other in the phenomenal world. He holds that the repeated occurrence of one event succeeding another event gives rise to the impression in us that there is a "constant conjunction" among the various events in the phenomenal world. As a result of this "constant conjunction", Hume holds that the mind forms a "habit" to expect upon the appearance of one event, the appearance of another event, which usually follows it. As a result of this, he explains that people tend to believe that there is a necessary connection among the various events in the world. This implies, according to Hume that necessary connection is only apparent and psychological and it is based on constant conjunction among the events. Thus he writes in the *Enquiries "...this idea of a necessary connexion among events arises from a number of similar instances which occur of constant conjunction of these events."*[4] He explains his position, through the example of two striking billiard balls. He writes, *"The first time a man saw the communication of motion by impulse, as by the shock of two billiard balls, he could not pronounce that the one event was connected, but only that it was conjoined with the other. After he has observed several instances of this nature, he then pronounces them to be connected."*[5] Thus Hume holds that one instance cannot give rise to an idea of the necessary connection but it is only a number of similar instances repeatedly experienced, which suggests the idea of necessary connection. He writes, *"...after a repetition of similar instances the mind is carried by habit, upon the appearance of one event, to expect its usual attendant and to believe that it will exist. This connexion, therefore, which we feel in the mind, this customary transition of the imagination from one object to its usual attendant, is the.... impression from which we form the idea of.... necessary connexion."*[6]

It thus follows that, for Hume there are no objective necessary connections in the material reality. He, on the other hand maintains that there is only a constant conjunction among the various events which are "loose and unconnected". He writes, *"...upon the whole there appears not, throughout all nature, any one instance of connexion which is conceivable by us. All events seen eventually loose and separate...They seem conjoined but never connected."*[7]

Hume thus expresses that necessary connection, is a product of custom, which is formed by observing several instances of constant conjunctions. In order to explain his position, he reverts to above example of two striking billiard balls. He argues that after observing a number of similar instances, the man... *"feels these events to be connected in his imagination, and can readily foretell the existence of one from the appearance of the other.*"[8]

It becomes apparent from the above statement of Hume that the idea of a necessary connexion, for him, occurs only in our thought. He spells out, *"When we say therefore, that one object is connected with another, we mean only that they have acquired a connexion in our thought, and give rise to this inference, by which they become proofs of each other's existence.*"[9]

Thus what is seen as a necessary connection among the events in the objective material reality, is taken by Hume to be "customary connexion" between one object and its "usual attendant", as it occurs in our "thought or imagination".

While attempting to explain away necessary connection through the concept of "custom", he writes, "...*whenever the repetition of any particular act or operation produces a propensity to renew the same act or operation, without being impelled by any reasoning or process of the understanding, we always say that this propensity is the effect of custom.*"[10] The necessary connection, which we observe in the phenomenal world, according to Hume is thus, a "propensity" which is produced by "custom" to pass from one object to the idea of its usual attendant. He says in the *Treatise "Upon the whole, necessity is something that exists in the mind, not in the objects,... necessity is nothing but that determination of the thought to pass from causes to effects, and from effects to causes, according to their experienced union.*"[11]

We thus find an element of subjectivity in Hume's

idea of "necessity" since he limits this idea to our thoughts and imagination.

While denying the idea of an objective necessary connection he sets forth in the *Enquiries*, "*When we look about us towards external objects and consider the operation of causes, we are never able, in a single instance, to discover any ... necessary connexion... which binds the effect to the cause, and renders the one an infallible consequence of the other. We only find, that the one does actually, in fact, follow the other... This is the whole that appears to the outward senses.*"[12] It follows according to Hume, that there are no "external impressions" which correspond to the idea of a necessary connection. Similarly, he asserts that no "internal impressions" can give rise to an idea of a necessary connection among the events. "*The mind feels no sentiment or inward impression from this succession of objects.*"[13]

In the absence of any "external" or "internal" impressions of a necessary connection, it logically follows, that for Hume, can be no idea of necessary connection among the events in the objective material reality. This is so, because, as we have already mentioned in our second chapter, while examining the nature of Hume's "impressions" and "ideas", that in Hume's ontology, there is no idea, which does not arise from a corresponding impression. He therefore explains that the idea of a necessary connection, is purely psychological and corresponding to it there is no objective truth. He concludes, "*Consequently, there is not, in any single... instance of cause and effect... anything which can suggest the idea of... necessary connexion.*"[14]

We thus find that for Hume, the idea of necessary connection has no objective significance. By denying a necessary causal relation, we find, that Hume, in the process also denies Locke's concept of "power" through which Locke explains the abstract idea of "cause" in his ontology. (This issue has been stated in the second chapter). While denying cause and effect as an `abstract' relation, Hume says, *"and as the power, by which one object produces another, is never discoverable merely from their idea, it is evident cause and effect are relations, of which we receive information not from any abstract reasoning or reflection."*[15] In this context while dismissing Locke's concept of cause as "power" he further writes, *"...the idea of production is the same with that of causation, and... no existence certainly and demonstratively implies a power in any other object."*[16]

It is thus entailed that the idea of a necessary connection is not an "abstract idea" and neither can it be `given' in our sense-experience.

It may be pointed out here that although Kant, also asserts that necessary connection is not given in sense-perception, he holds that this idea is known a-priori. He does not make "causation" a subjective issue like Hume. For him the idea of necessary connection is inherent in the concept of cause *"...the very concept of a cause so manifestly contains the concept of a necessity of connection...."*[17] Kant explains that any attempt to derive the idea of necessary connection from empirical experience, implies a subjective necessity. So he maintains that even though causal necessity is known a-priori, it has an objective significance. Kant's criticism of Hume's subjective view of causation is extendable to that of Ayer's, since the latter's view of causation is based on Hume's concept of causation. We shall take up this issue in the ensuing section of our present chapter.

Hume's view of causation thus appears to us, to be diametrically opposed to the scientific view of causation.

The scientific view of causation assumes an objective reality where all the events of the natural and social reality are causally interconnected. Since Hume denies the objective material reality, he consequently denies the idea of objective necessary connection among the various events in the reality. He argues that in any moment, whatever experience tells us can be best expressed as relation between two events consistently obtained in the past. But this leads to the problem of induction in Hume's system. He formulates the principle of induction in the *Treatise* where he writes, *"...instances of which we have had no experience, must resemble those of which we have had experience, and that the course of nature continues always uniformly the same."*[18]

But the question arises can Hume justify the principle of the "uniformity of nature" within his ontological frame work?

Hume maintains that *"uniformity of nature" is not demonstratively justifiable. This is because, he holds that we may come across a "change" in the course of the nature, which may prove that "such a change is not absolutely impossible."*[19]

We thus find that in Hume's ontology, the judgement, namely that "course of nature remains uniformly the same" is a probable judgement. He holds that all probable reasoning or all the judgements of probability are based on our past experiences. According to him probable reasoning proceed from something which is already present in the mind, either "seen" or "remembered", from which one infers some other thing "connected with it, which is not seen or remembered". He writes, *"...probability is founded on the presumption of a resemblance betwixt those objects of which we have had experience, and those of which we have had none; and, therefore, it is impossible this presumption can arise from probability."*[20] This implies that induction can be proved only in sense-experience through our past experiences. It thus follows that the inferences on which we base our beliefs about empirical matters are not formally valid. Even the conclusions that we arrive at cannot be shown to be probable without arguing in a circle. Thus inferences based on induction cannot be demonstratively justified in Hume's ontology. For him such inferences result only from our habit. In other words, all the propositions of natural and social sciences remain mere probabilities for Hume.

Let us now examine and compare Ayer's view of causation with that of Hume's.

AYER'S VIEW OF CAUSATION

In his analysis of causation, Ayer uses the formal mode of speech, as opposed to Hume's material mode of speech. He analyses causal relations or causal connections in terms of causal statements or causal judgements. We have already discussed while dealing with the epistemology and ontology of Hume and Ayer that although both these philosophers claim to differ with regard to their basic objectives, Ayer's philosophical position is a reiteration of the ontological and epistemological assumptions of Hume. And this also applies in the case of his analysis of causation.

Ayer maintains that causation is a "correlation" which is given in sense experience, that it is based on our "attitude" and that there are no necessary connections between two contiguously existing events. He holds that every assertion of a causal connection, is an expression of a "causal law" of the form "C causes E", where C and E represent classes of events, and it is "equivalent to a proposition of the form whenever C, then E".

Since events are nothing but sense-data in Ayer's ontology, therefore, we find that he tries to explain away the causal laws in terms of "conjunction of sense-data". These sense-data as we have already seen are not of single determinate kind but they belong to a "relatively indeterminate range". Because of this, Ayer envisages the "law" or universal causation as a "hypothesis" which, according to him, is based on the "actual observation of the concurrences of sensible events". Even though the concept of "law" is a "hypothesis" for Ayer, like Hume, he assumes that we *"believe" in this law because "this belief is derived from our guiding principle that... the future course of our sensations will be in accordance with the past."*[21] Ayer's concept of "causal law" is thus based on a correlation of past and future sensations, which is also implicated in Hume's account of causation, as stated earlier.

We have also shown in the context of Hume that the above mentioned correlation is based on our "habit", as well as on our "imagination". In confirmity with Hume,

Ayer also maintains that every causal relation is based on an "imaginative arrangement of facts". In this context while analysing causal relations or causal connections as "causal statements", he writes in *Probability and Evidence*, "*Like other statements which trade on the concept of law, causal statements are only partly factual. For the rest, they exhibit our arrangements of facts and the extensions of these arrangements to imaginary instances.*"[22] Thus Ayer claims that causal statements are partly factual and partly based on our mental habits.

He says that the "factual content" of causal statements depends "on the level at which they operate". The factual contents thus imply Ayer's sense-data or sense-contents which are `given in sense experience'. In other words, we finds that what Ayer calls "factual generalizations" are nothing but generalizations of the sense-data. He holds that such a generalization may be a "universal generalization", and at the same time it may also be a "statement of tendency". The distinction between the two, according to him, depends on our "attitude" towards them. He attempts to explain the "statement of tendency" through "human affairs" It seems to us that since he reduces "human affairs" into "bodily behaviour" and further the body into the "actual and possible sense-data", (as mentioned in our fourth chapter) the "statements of tendency", like the universal generalizations consist of nothing but the generalizations of sense-data in Ayer's ontology.

Ayer further holds that all the universal generalisations of law are not causal. For example he excludes functional laws like the law connecting the temperature, volume and pressure of a gas, and taxonomic laws, like the laws that describe which insects are deciduous, from the domain of causal laws. He classifies the causal statements into four main categories and claims that none of them represent a necessary causal law.

According to him the first category of causal statements consists of the generalisations of law or fact that could be explained by means of a "wider theory". In such cases, Ayer holds that the term which is used to "encapsulate" the theory is taken to designate the cause of the phenomena with which a generalisation deals. *"The first class consists of the cases where a generalisation, whether of fact or of law, is explained by means of a wider theory, and some term which is intended to encapsulate the theory is taken to designate the cause of the phenomena with which the generalisation deals. It is in this large sense that we speak of the effects of gravitation or of electricity."*[23]

The second category of "causal statements", according to him, include as "cause", all such cases in which the nature of a thing is explained on the basis of its properties. For example, a piece of elastic stretches because it is made of rubber. Through this category of "causal statements", Ayer explains our use of the word "because".

The third category, according to him deals with cases of causality in which the state of one's own mental condition is the cause of his behaviour. "Thirdly, there are the cases in which a disposition, or a state of mind, is said to be the cause of its manifestations. Thus a man may be said to yawn because he is bored.... *Such statements are not trivial as they sometimes are thought to be. They fit the manifestation into a wider pattern.*"[24]

Finally, Ayer holds that there are causal statements which link two states of affairs at the "same observational or theoretical level". And this category of causal statements, according to him, is the most philosophical significant category.

We find that this last category of "causal statements" refers to Hume's relation of "succession" and "contiguity" among events with which he tries to explain away the necessary causal connections in his ontology.

Ayer argues that mere contiguity among the existing events does not make it a necessary causal connection. He attempts to illustrate his position on the basis of the following observation in *Probability and Evidence*. He holds that sometimes we are forced to say that flowers in the garden died because the gardener forgot to water the plants. But he asks, why should we blame the gardener to have caused the death of flowers?, when any one would have watered the plants, so that they could have survived. Ayer says that the immediate response may be that gardener is expected to do so. This is the reason why he maintains, we identify him (gardener) as the cause of the flowers death. "*This example illustrates our tendency to fasten on to a condition which deviates from the norm. Presumably, the flowers would have survived if anyone had watered them, not just the gardener; but because the gardener was expected to do it, his omission is singled out.*"[25] On the basis of the above example, Ayer tries to show that it is insufficient to represent causality as a relation between events. He reverts to the gardener's inaction in the above example and holds that it cannot be taken as an event. Thus for him, two contiguously existing events cannot give rise to the idea of a necessary connection. It appears to us that the above mentioned view follows from his pluralist ontology. As we have already discussed in the preceding chapter that ontologically what exists for Ayer are the sense-data. These sense-data are discrete, unconnected sensory units. Consequently they project events or states of affairs which are equally unconnected.

While denying the necessary connection, Ayer explains in the *Foundations of Empirical Knowledge*, "*No doubt the use of the word "cause" does to most minds vaguely convey a suggestion that events in some way compel one another to occur. But this... is the legacy of a discarded metaphysic which can survive in a `scientific' concept only as a more or less misleading metaphor*."[26] In attempting to further negate the idea of "necessity" he says "*...to those who speak as if there were necessity in the nature is whether they really mean to imply that the laws of nature are normative rule, enforced by a divine will. If they do not mean to imply this, their talk of necessity is at best an unfortunate... metaphor*."[27]

It is clearly evident from the above account that for Ayer, the belief in necessary causal laws is a matter of blind faith. We thus find that, necessary causal laws do not have any objective significance in his ontology. On the other hand he argues that cause and effect are nothing but what we "choose" them to be. He writes, "*causes are what we choose them to be. We do not decide what facts habitually go together but we do decide what combination are to be imaginatively projected*."[28]

The above account smacks of subjectivity in Ayer's

analysis of causation, as we also find it in the context of Hume. "Causation" for him is therefore a psychological issue and it has no implication in the objective material world. In denying the idea of necessary causal connection, it logically follows that Ayer denies like Hume, Locke's abstract idea of the relation of causation, based on "power".

A question arises now, that if there are no necessary causal connections, can Ayer justify the principle of induction in his ontology? Ayer, like Hume, makes an attempt to tackle, this problem through the principle of the "uniformity of nature". But he argues that even this principle is based on a misleading assumption that the "past experience holds good for the future". He writes, "*...it is often said, that we can justify induction by invoking the uniformity of nature.... But, in fact, the principle of the uniformity of nature merely states, in a misleading fashion, the assumption that past experience is a reliable guide to the future....*"[29]

He further argues that there is no guarantee that nature will not surprise us any time. "*...if there were a law of universal causation, a sufficient knowledge of the antecedents of any event would enable us to predict its occurrence. There may still be surprise in store for us because we neither know all the relevant facts, nor have we yet discovered all the laws which govern them.*"[30]

We thus find that Ayer is dubious about the problem of induction. He believes that if there is a law of univrsal causation then we should be able to predict the consequences of any event whatsoever. However he argues that inspite of these predictions being genuine, we are always surprised if our much expected predictions are not true. This is mainly because we fail to discover the laws that govern them except their law-like character which is observable. Thus like Hume, Ayer concludes that inductive generalisations are highly probable.

In Agreement with Hume, he also maintains that probability of a proposition itself is based on past experiences which increases our "confidence". *"Roughly speaking, all that we mean by saying that an observation increases the probability of a proposition is that it increases our confidence in the proposition.... And, similarly, to say of an observation that it diminishes the probability of a proposition is to say that it decreases our willingness to include the proposition in the system of accepted hypotheses which serve us as guides to the future."*[31]

This implies that the degree in the increase or decrease of probability of a particular proposition if a matter of fact, depends on its occurrence which is given in sensory-experience. Thus Ayer seems to justify the Humean conception that the principle of induction cannot be proved unless it is given in sense-experience.

We may briefly state here the various senses of probability as recognized by Ayer and other logical positivists and discussed by K. Srinivas in his book. *An Evaluation of A.J. Ayer's Logical Positions.*[32] These are:

(1) a-priori calculus

(2) frequency theory, and

(3) the logical theory and statements of credibility.

Ayer illustrates the "a-priori calculus" as the gamblers

theory of probability through which gamblers predict certain results. For example the probability of throwing double six with a true dice is 1/36. According to Ayer this relates to the mathematical calculus of chances. It does not in itself leads us to any conclusion about the likelihood of any event. Thus, he holds that such a theory is not used by the scientists to test his hypotheses.

The "frequency theory", on the other hand, is a "statistical statement", according to Ayer. He illustrates this kind of probability, through the example of the probability of an unborn infant. This kind of a distribution theory of probability, according to Ayer, is a model worked out scientifically to predict certain future events.

Finally, the "logical theory" of probability according to him, consists of "statements of credibility". For example he holds, "it is probable that the economic union of Europe will lead to political union within the next half-century." We may replace this example by an example in the Indian context that there is a probability that the unity in opposition parties in India will throw the ruling party out of power. This implies according to Ayer that, "we have reason to feel at least more confident than not that such an such an event will come about." He further maintains that these statements may be based upon statistical statements, but they are not themselves statistical.

On the basis of the above three instances of probability, Srinivas tries to show that the concept of probability does not play any role in establishing the existence of certain laws of nature.

But we find that Ayer, on the other hand, applies the

concept of probability to all the statements of law without recognising their objective significance in the course of scientific investigation.

To sum up, our present chapter we may say that Hume's and Ayer's views of causation rest on the "mental" arrangements of certain events that are given in sense experience. As a result causation does not have any objective significance in their ontology. It is only a `subjective' talk of certain phenomena that takes place in nature. The denial of necessary causal connection is therefore a logical outcome of the pluralist ontology of both Hume and Ayer.

Suman Gupta interprets that in a pluralist ontology, one can only have 'external relations' and 'no internal relations'. She explains that in a pluralist ontology there is no scope of any interpenetration among the various events of the reality. The whole remains 'identical' in nature and one cannot observe any change and consequently any development in the natural and social reality. In this regard she writes, "*From the ontological point of view we should say that the denial of the existence of material substance by Hume and Ayer logically implies pluralism. And pluralism, in its turn, assumes external relations. External relations are opposed to internal relations.... External relations imply that the objects or phenomena which stand to one another in terms of external relations and constitute a whole remain exactly the same, retain their identical nature irrespective of whether they are inside or outside the whole. That is, they do not penetrate into one another. The whole is simply a sum total of the isolated and discrete units. On the other hand, the supposition that there are internal relations implies that different objects and phenomena are... various aspects of a totality and they penetrate into one another....*"[33] Thus, it seems to follow that in the absence of these basic aspects of an objective material reality, one cannot have the notion of a necessary causal connection both in the case of Hume as well as Ayer.

If the concept of "causation" is however, analysed from a scientific point of view, we find that cause and effect constitute a necessary connection. In other words causality, in this sense, is based on a chain of reciprocal connections, where each link serves both as a cause as well as an effect. This implies that the connection between cause and effect is internal and is consequently `law-governed' in character. This is called determinism. But since Hume and Ayer both deny the necessary causal connections, and explain the development of phenomenona through habit *i.e.,* through consciousness, their position is one of indeterminism. Their approach to causality can therefore be interpreted as an `idealist' approach.

Since a necessary causal connection is denied by both Hume and Ayer, Suman Gupta argues that consequently one cannot have universal and necessary knowledge of the "matters of fact" in the philosophical systems of these philosophers. "*...if every event is discrete unit then there cannot be necessary connection. In that case there cannot be universal and necessary knowledge of the empirical world. And in the context of causality this is precisely what Hume and Ayer advocated.* "[34]

REFERENCES

1. David Hume, *A Treatise of Human Nature*, vol.I Introduction by A.D. Lindsay) (London, 1981), pp. 78-79.

2. *Ibid.*, p. 79.
3. *Ibid.*
4. David Hume, *Enquiries*, L.A.Selby-Bigge (ed.), 3rd edn. (Oxford, 1975), p. 75.
5. *Ibid.*
6. *Ibid.*
7. *Ibid.*, p. 74.
8. *Ibid.*, pp. 75-76.
9. *Ibid.*, p. 76.
10. *Ibid.*, p. 43.
11. David Hume, *A Treatise*, *op.cit.*, pp. 163-4.
12. David Hume, *Enquiries*, *op.cit.*, p. 63.
13. *Ibid.*
14. *Ibid.*, p. 63.
15. David Hume, *Treatise*, *op.cit.*, p. 73.
16. *Ibid.*, p. 93.
17. Immanuel Kant, *Critique of Pure Reason* (London, 1973), p. 27.
18. David Hume, *Treatise*, *op.cit.*, p. 91.
19. *Ibid.*
20. *Ibid.*, p.92.
21. A.J. Ayer, *Language, Truth and Logic* (Hormondsworth, 1975), p.131.
22. A.J. Ayer, *Probability and Evidence* (London, 1973), p.132.

23. *Ibid.*, p. 133.

24. *Ibid.*

25. *Ibid.*, p. 134.

26. A.J. Ayer, *Foundations of Empirical Knowledge* (London, 1971), p. 183.

27. *Ibid.*, p. 198.

28. A.J. Ayer, *Probability and Evidence*, *op.cit.*, p. 139.

29. A.J. Ayer, *Language, Truth and Logic*, *op.cit.*, p. 66.

30. A.J. Ayer, *The Central Questions of Philosophy* (Harmondsworth, 1976), p.161.

31. A.J. Ayer, *Language, Truth and Logic*, *op.cit.*, p. 132.

32. K. Srinivas "An Evaluation of A.J. Ayer's Logical Positivism" (New Delhi, 1990), pp. 110-11.

33. Suman Gupta, *Twentieth Century Philosophy* (Bangalore, 1991), p. 51.

34. *Ibid,* pp. 51-52.

6

CONCLUSION: A COMPARATIVE ACCOUNT OF HUME AND AYER

While discussing the epistemological and ontological doctrines of David Hume and A.J. Ayer, we have arrived at the conclusion, that, the empiricism of both these philosophers can be traced from some of the assumptions of Descartes dualism. Descartes, as a rationalist, assumes that mind and matter do not interact and that mind can directly know only its ideas. It has been shown, that, for the exception of Locke, who, endeavours to propound the above mentioned dualism through empiricism and thus commits contradictions, Berkeley, as well as Hume and Ayer take for granted only the mental side of Cartesian dualism.

In Berkeley's philosophy, this becomes evident through his acceptance of both the finite and the infinite minds in his ontology. His philosophical position is therefore one of idealism, because the nature of ultimate reality, is mental in his case. At the same time we have also shown that it is subjective. This is because, he avows that the ideas, for their existence, depend on the perceiving minds. We therefore find that Berkeley advocates subjective-idealism through empiricism. But in the final analysis it may also be said that the distinction between subjective and objective idealism, does not hold valid for Berkeley. This aspect of his philosophy is highlighted by Suman Gupta in *The Origin and Theories of Linguistic Philosophy*. Suman Gupta puts forward the opinion that *"it is not the ideas but the spiritual substance which he regarded as the ultimate reality. That is to say that the spiritual substance can exist independently of the ideas but ideas cannot exist independently of the spiritual substance."*[1] So, we find that Berkeley's position in the last analysis can be regarded as an objective idealist one.

On the basis of Berkeley's subjective-idealist premise, namely, "to exist is to be perceived", it seems to us that Hume can also be interpreted as a subjective-idealist, as has been argued by some philosophers. Although in his philosophical system, the "impressions" and "ideas" unlike Berkeley's "ideas", exist, without the existence of a "spiritual substance" or "soul", we have shown that they can be regarded as `mental' like the `sensations' of Berkeley, since they are `abstracted from the concrete objective reality'.

In a similar strain, Ayer, who is an analytic philosopher, and belongs to the logical positivism school of linguistic philosophy, is also treated as a subjective-idealist philosopher. This is because, through his method of 'analysis' he denies the 'objective' material reality, and asserts the existence only of one's own sense-data or sense-contents. These "sense-data" being "private" thus resemble the 'sensations' of Berkeley. Since, the 'sensations', however 'abstract', they may be, cannot exist without a mind, we have shown through relevant arguments that Ayer irrespective of his claims logically 'assumes' a mental substance. It is for this reason, that we say that both these philosophers, as empiricists take for granted Descarte's mental substance. In this sense we also find that Berkeley's subjective-idealism is reflected in the philosophies of Hume and Ayer.

Ayer's 'analysis' of linguistic concepts is therefore based on certain ontological presuppositions of both Berkeley and Hume. Broadly speaking we have tried to show that he restates most of Hume's central doctrines by using a formal mode of speech.

To this effect Ayer himself says, *"So far as their positivism went they were continuing an old philosophical tradition - it is remarkable how many of their most radical doctrines are already to be found in Hume."*[2]

Starting from his classification of meaningful propositions into 'analytic' and 'synthetic', we find that it is based on Hume's division of knowledge between "Relations of ideas" and "Matters of fact". Following Hume, he categorises, the propositions of mathematics and logic as analytic propositions. His synthetic propositions on the other hand are assertions about the existents. Thus like Hume, Ayer also 'separates' the rational aspect of knowledge from its empirical base. For him, the ultimate reality consists of only the "sense-data" or the "sense-contents" like the "impressions" of Hume. He arrives at this position on the basis of his well-known "verification principle of meaning". These sense-contents, according to Ayer, are not objects, but what he calls 'part of sense-experience'. Being part of sense-experience, they are interpreted as 'mental' entities, like the 'impressions' of Hume. We thus find, that like Hume, Ayer too, identifies the objects of knowledge with the source of knowledge.

In the context of the material substance and the "self" we come across a reductive analysis, in Ayer's ontology, just as we find in Hume's case.

He reduces 'the material objects' into 'logical constructions out of actual and possible sense-data.' just as Hume 'reduces' them into "bundle of impressions and ideas". The 'possible sense-data' in Ayer's ontology play the same role as the category of "ideas" in Hume. That is, to say, Ayer introduces the 'possible sense data', in order, precisely to explain the unperceived existence of material objects. And in line with Hume, he also uses certain "laws of sensory experience", in his attempt to "construct" the objects in the external material world.

Similarly, we find that Ayer completely agrees with Hume's arguments, for the denial of mental substance. In this context he says, *"Our reasoning on this point, as on so many others, is in conformity with Hume's. He too, rejected notion of substantive ego on the ground that no such entity was observable."*[3] Thus we see that for Ayer `self' is a "logical construction out of sense-experiences, which constitute the actual and possible sense-history of a self." And the way Hume attempts to explain "self" through the concept of "memory" and "personal identity". Ayer attempts to do so by introducing the concept of "bodily identity" in his ontology. But since for Ayer `body' is nothing but a "collection of these sense data", hence we find that there is no major change in Ayer's position from that of Hume's on this particular issue.

It follows from their phenomenalistic interpretation of substance that the distinction between the appearances and the reality is abolished by both these philosophers. In their respective ontologies, one finds only the appearances and the particulars, which are discrete and transitory. Their ontological position is thus one which embodies pluralism.

We therefore find that Hume's position, on induction and causation, namely, that science is nothing but regularities of occurrences and that predictions about the future, can only be made on past occurrences, is reflected in Ayer's view on causation and induction. By denying, necessary causal connections, Ayer, like Hume, fails to account for scientific knowledge. For him, as for Hume, scientific knowledge consists of only an arrangement and ordering of the various sense-data. It is, therefore, only "probable" and not certain for them.

In the light of the above mentioned, overall view of the basic epistemological and ontological positions of Hume and Ayer, we in conclusion have argued that the approach which is adopted both by Hume as well as Ayer, is based on premises which are objectively untenable. Proceeding from the premise that our own sense-experiences constitute the whole body of knowledge, Hume maintains that one cannot have knowledge of the existence of anything other than the 'impressions'; and, similarly Ayer concludes from the same premise that one can have a knowledge, only of the sense-contents or the sense-data. These very claims of both Hume and Ayer are subject to serious criticisms, as they provide one-side picture of reality.

It is certain that we cannot have knowledge solely by concentrating on these sensations. Knowledge in our view is the knowledge of objective reality wherein all the aspects are dialectically related *i.e.,* follow internal relations and exist independently of human cognition. In other worlds we want to assert that knowledge is not to be limited to sense-perceptions alone. It involves reasoning contexts (Lewis), practical applications of theorics etc. But where Hume and Ayer are concerned they seem to equate knowledge with each individual's private sensations. Since what is "private" cannot be communicated their approach seems to generate solipsistic tendencies in their philosophies. Thus their analysis of knowledge is one-sided and reflects idealism and absolutism. This aspect is brought about by Suman Gupta in her book *Twentieth Century Philosophy.* In this context she quotes A.P.Sheptulin where he writes, "*Exaggerating any aspect of knowledge, depriving it of its bonds with its other aspects and with matter, and absolutising it inevitably lead to idealism. The epistemological roots of Idealism lie therefore in making an absolute of some aspect or peculiarity of the process of cognition, which leads to one-sided interpretation and distortion of it... sensations and perceptions are the forms of sense knowledge that depend on man, his nervous system... experience, and the like. If, however, we... forget that sensations and perceptions depend not only on man, but also on the objects influencing his sense-organs,... we come inevitably to subjectivism, i.e., we shall affirm that the content of sensations and perceptions is determined by the subject (man), which will bring us to idealism....*"[4]

Contrary to Hume's and Ayer's views, we assert that knowledge is not private property of one's own mind. It is a social product and is acquired through the combination of various skills. Knowledge in our view is inseparably built up by each individual's effort and is social and public by nature. In this context Suman Gupta while interpreting knowledge to be a conscious activity writes, *"The very process of knowledge implies that it is a conscious activity. It is the ideal reflection of the surrounding world in man's consciousness. But what is being reflected are... the essential causal connections in the objective reality. In other words, knowledge goes beyond the appearances to the essence of things. That is, knowledge is not confined to sensory perceptions but it is concerned with the formulation of theories which have objective content."*[5]

We thus find that the theories which are propounded by Hume and Ayer towards knowledge acquisition lacks sufficiency and completion when they elevate impressions and sense data into all sufficient and supporting explanation for knowledge. In the name of eliminating metaphysics both these philosopher, by giving supremacy to sensations in the acquisition of knowledge, themselves advocate a metaphysical position.

As far as nature and content of science is concerned, the utility of scientific knowledge is not at all acknowledged by these philosophers. For them scientific knowledge is only ordering of one's own sensatiosn through external relation. Both Hume and Ayer deny the necessary causal relations which are inherent in nature.

We on the other hand feel that scientific knowledge is highely conceptiualised and derives from interconnectiosn among the various aspects of reality. In fact these interconnections provide theoretical basis for scientific knowledge which is put into practice by the scientists in order to transaform reality for the progress of mankind.

Looking from this angle, the epistemological consequences of Hume and Ayer appear to us to be incompatible with scientific proofs.

Suman Gupta holds that by denying the necessary causal connections in the objective reality Hume and Ayer denied the very 'foundations of science.'

In spite of the fact that Hume's empiricism and Ayer's logical positivism stand in glaring contradiction to actual scientific proof, both these philosophers are credited with posing a number of interesting problems that are common to philosophers as well as scientists. Our intention in this thesis, has been, mainly to show, that the crisis in the philosophies of Hume and Ayer are brought about by inadequacy of their epistemological and ontological structures.

REFERENCES

1. Suman Gupta, *Origin and Theories of Linguistic Philosophy* (New Delhi, 1983), p.49.

2. A.J. Ayer, "The Vienna Circle", in A.J. Ayer (ed.), *The Revolution in Philosophy* (London, 1963), p.71.

3. A.J. Ayer, *Language, Truth and Logic* (Harmondsworth, 1975), p.167.

4. A.P. Sheptulin, Fundamentals of Marxist Philosophy, quoted in Suman Gupta, *Twentieth Century Philosophy* (Bangalore, 1991), pp. 39-40.
5. *Ibid*, pp. 41-42.

BIBLIOGRAPHY

PRIMARY SOURCES

Ayer, A.J., and others (eds.), *The Revolution in Philosophy* (London: Macmillan, 1963).

Ayer, A.J., *Philosophical Essays* (London: Macmillan, 1965)

Ayer, A.J. and Winch, R. (eds.), *British Empirical Philosophers Locke, Berkeley, Hume, Reid and J.S.Mill* (New York: A Clarion Book, 1968).

Ayer, A.J., *The Foundations of Empirical Knowledge* (London: Macmillan and Co.Ltd., 1971).

-------, *The Concept of a Person and Other Essays* (London: Macmillan, 1973).

--------, *Metaphysics and Commonsense* (London: Macmillan, 1973).

--------, *Probability and Evidence* (London: Macmillan, 1973).

--------, *The Origins of Pragmatism* (London: Macmillan, 1974).

--------, *Language, Truth and Logic* (Harmondsworth: Penguin Book, 1975), 2nd edn.

--------, *Hume* (London: Oxford University Press, 1980).

Ayer, A.J., *The Central Questions of Philosophy* (Penguin Books, 1981).

--------, *Philosophy in the Twentieth Century* (London: Unwin Paper backs, 1984).

--------, *The Problem of Knowledge* (Harmondsworth: Penguin Books, 1984).

Hume, David, *A Treatise of Human Nature*, "Introduction", by A.D. Linday (London: J.M. Dent and Sons Ltd., New York: Dutton and Co. Inc., 1961), vol.I.

--------, *A Treatise of Human Nature*, Earnest C. Mossner (ed.) (Baltimore: Penguin Books, 1969).

-------, *An Enquiry Concerning Human Understanding* (Glasgow: Fontana/Collins, 1975), Appendix B.

-------, *Enquiries,* Selby-Bigge, L.A. (ed.) (Oxford: Clarendon Press, 1975), 3rd edition.

Hume, David, *A Treatise of Human Nature*, MacNabb, D.G.C. (ed.) (Glasgow: Fontana/Collins, 1978) Book I.

SECONDARY SOURCES

Books

Ackermann, Robert, *Theories of Knowledge: A Critical Introduction* (New York: Megra Hill, 1974).

Afanasyev, V., *Marxist Philosophy* (Moscow: Progress Publishers, 1968).

Berkeley, George, *The Principles of Human Knowledge*, edited and introduced by G.J. Warnock (Glasgow: Collins/Fontana, 1975).

Chisholm, Roderick M., *Theory of Knowledge* (New Delhi: Prentice-Hall of India Pvt. Ltd., 1977).

Copleston, Frederick, S.J., *A History of Philosophy* (London: Burns Oates and Wash Bourne Limited, 1959), vol.V.

Cornforth, Maurice, *Science and Idealism* (New York: International Publishers, 1947).

-------, *In Defence of Philosophy Against Positivism and Pragmatism* (London: Lawrence and Wishart, 1950).

Dancy, J., *Berkeley: An Introduction* (New York: Basil Blackwell, 1987), p.11.

Datta, D.M., *The Chief Currents of Contemporary Philosophy* (Patna: Bharati Bhawan, 1972).

Descartes, Rene, *Discourse on Method and the Meditations* (Harmondsworth: Penguin Books, 1979).

Ewing, A.C., *The Fundamental Questions of Philosophy* (Bombay: Allied Publishers, 1967).

Flage, Daniel E., *David Hume's Theory of Mind* (London and New York: Routledge, 1990).

Foster, John, *A.J. Ayer: The Arguments of the Philosophers*, Ted Honderich (ed.) (London: Routledge and Kegan Paul, 1985).

Gower, Barry (ed.), *Logical Positivism in Perspective: Essays on Language, Truth and Logic* (London: Croom Helm, 1987).

Gross, Barry R., *Analytic Philosophy: An Historical Introduction* (New Delhi: Oxford and IBH Publishing Co).

Gupta, Suman, *The Origin and Theories of Linguistic Philosophy (A Marxist Point of View)* (New Delhi: Intellectual Publishing House, 1983).

-------, *A Critique of Wittgenstein* (New Delhi: Intellectual Publishing House, 1986).

-------, *Twentieth Century Philosophy* (Bangalore: Nava Karnataka Publications Private Limited, 1991).

-------, *Man, Science and Social Progress*, Puchala Satyanarayana (ed.) (Kakinada: R.K.Ideological and Philosophical Institute, 1995).

Harris, E.E., *Nature, Mind and Modern Science* (New York: Humanities Press, George Allen and Unwin).

Hospers, John, *An Introduction to Philosophical Analysis* (New Delhi: Allied Publishers Pvt.Ltd., 1971).

Kant, Immanuel, *Critique of Pure Reason*, Norman Kemp Smith (trans.) (London: Macmillan, 1973).

Locke, John, *An Essay Concerning Human Understanding*, Abridged and edited with an introduction by John W. Yolton (London: Dent, 1976).

Macdonald, G.F. (ed.), *Perception and Identity: Essays Presented to A.J.Ayer with His Replies to Them* (London: The Macmillan Press Ltd., 1979).

Macdonald, G. and Wright, C. (eds.), *Fact, Science and Morality - Essays on A.J.Ayer's Language, Truth and Logic* (New York: Basil Blackwell, 1986).

Mill, John Stuart, *System of Logic* (London and Colchester: Spottiswoode, Ballantyne, 1965).

Novack, George, *Empiricism and Its Evolution: A Marxist Point of View* (New York: Pathfinders Press Inc., 1971).

Passamore, John, *A Hundred Years of Philosophy* (Harmondsworth: Penguin Books, 1968).

--------, *Hume's Intentions* (Duckworth, 1980), 3rd edn.

Price, H.H., *Perception* (London: Mathuen and Co., 1961), 2nd edn.

Russell, Bertrand, *Problems of Philosophy* (London: Philosophical Library, 1912).

--------, *History of Western Philosophy* (London: Unwin Paper, 1979).

Sheptulin, A.P., *Marxist-Leninist Philosophy* (Moscow: Progress Publishers, 1980).

Srinivas, K. *An Evaluation and A.J. Ayer's Logical Positivism* (New Delhi, IPH, 1990)

Strawson, Gallen, *The Secret Connection, Causation, Realism and David Hume* (Oxford: Oxford Clarendon Press, 1989).

Wright, John P., *The Sceptical Realism of David Hume* (Manchester: Manchester University Press, 1983).

Articles

Berlin, Isaiah Sir, "Empirical Propositions and Hypothetical Statements', *Mind*, N.S. (London), vol.59, no.59, 1950, pp.289-322.

Church, Alonzo, "Review of the second edition of Language,

Truth and Logic", *Journal of Symbolic Logic* (London), vol.14, 1949, pp.52-53.

Cornforth, Maurice, "Is Analysis, a Useful Method in Philosophy", *Proceedings of the Aristotelian Society Supplement*, N.S. (London), vol.40, no.13, 1934, pp.90-118.

Gupta, Suman, "Linguistic Philosophy: Its Social Implications", *Journal of the School of Languages - Language and Literature in Society* (New Delhi), vol.5, no.1 & 2, Monsoon 1977, Winter 1977-78.

-------, "Bertrand Russell and A.J.Ayer: A Dialectico Materialist Approach", *Marxian Sociology* (New Delhi), vol.2, 1979.

-------, "A.J.Ayer: A Loss to the World of Philosophy", *Journal of the School of Languages - Structures of Significance*, vol.2, 1991.

Wisdon, John, "Metaphysics and Verification", *Mind*, N.S., vol.47, no.47, 1938, pp.356-60.